Title: *A Life in the Political Wilderness*

Author: Welf Herfurth

© Finis Mundi Press, 2011
© Welf Herfurth, 2011

Cover picture: Hildr Jørgensen
Proofreader: Keith Preston

Finis Mundi Press
http://finismundipress.blogspot.com

ISBN: 978-989-8336-27-9
Copyright Deposit: 332403/11

A record copy of this book is available at the
Portuguese National Library.

Finis Mundi is a registered trademark of Antagonista Editora (Portugal)

A Life in the Political Wilderness
By Welf Herfurth

Finis Mundi Press

For Narelle - Thank you for being the great partner you are.

CONTENTS

ACKNOWLEDGMENTS

In my journeys through the political wilderness I have encountered many outstanding men and women, too many to mention them all here, who helped me to form my political beliefs and challenged my views. Many are still a major part of my life.

Unfortunately, it is with great regret that in today's political climate many of them cannot be named with their real names here because their involvement with me and the politics we are caught up in can seriously impact their life. So you National Anarchists here in Australia, the guys from the Nationalist Alternative and all the people in Melbourne, Perth, Adelaide and Sydney who know me and worked with me – A big thank you for all your input and suggestions. I know that we didn't agree on everything all the time, but that is what makes your friendship so special. You are champions....

Some of the people I can thank by name are Pen & Andy, Matt & Karen; James, Doug, Jeff, Dave, Chris, Dr James Saleam, Prof Andrew Frazer, David Oldfield and his lovely wife, Hildr from Tasmania, Nick from Perth, Jim from Towoombba, Andrew Yeoman from San Francisco, Wolfgang Bendel from Germany.....

And I especially thank Troy Southgate for being the inspiration in my life that you are. I do not think you know what impact you have on people's lives, especially mine.......

And last, but not least, to all the people in the world that fight for what they believe in against systems that believe that we are just tools. Your fight and struggle inspires me every day and makes me feel humble as you are do

Welf Herfurth

INTRODUCTION

It is my great pleasure to introduce to you the work of Welf Herfurth, a man that I am proud to describe as both a friend and a comrade. The thirteen essays contained in this volume deal with a range of diverse and illuminating subjects, including Race, Class, Politics, Economics, Anarchism and Revolution. They will surprise you, perhaps even shock you. But if that is what is required in order to shake you from your lethargy, or perhaps allow those who are already motivated to some degree to understand precisely what must now be done to salvage what remains of our racial and cultural identity, then so be it.

The style of Welf's literary excursions match his politics. Indeed, whilst his articles deal with issues pertaining to chaos and decline, his characteristic German temperament means, inevitably, that he is not merely able to structure his work in a clear and concise format, but can also offer a series of workable solutions that bring order and sanity to those circumstances which often appear wholly intractable or irreversible. As a calm and level-headed realist, therefore, Welf has the ability to convert theory into praxis. He understands only too well that dynamic action, born of a keen intellect, must be unleashed with careful precision until it hits its selected target with all the power and fury of a thunderbolt.

Basic common sense, which, for many people, is presently hidden from view like a bright sun caught behind a black cloud, is therefore made visible and apparent. Welf is a voice in the wilderness; a teacher for our times; a maker and a shaper, a bastion of sanity in an increasingly dangerous and unpredictable world; and a defiant and indomitable prophet who is ready to meet the socio-economic apocalypse that waits for us in the shadows like a ravenous wolf. You would do well to heed his warnings, to acquaint yourself with his ideas, and to act accordingly.

Troy Southgate
East Sussex
Summer 2011

PREFACE

Some people are natural born leaders. Some are crooks by birth and by genes. Some have a knack for musical and artistic expression. Welf Herfurth has remained faithful to the ancient Germanic tradition of a Kulturtraeger, a "culture bearer," a trade once highly praised among thinkers and poets in Europe, and which played an enormous importance in shaping the cultural battlefield stretching from the late 18th century to the first half of the 20th century. Attempting to understand serial catastrophes that befell the Occident after 1945, one must first become acquainted with the metaphysical meaning of the role of cultural bearers. Culture bearing, or what came to be known later on in Germany as Kulturkampf ("culture war") has always been an essential element in the politics of power. Alas, spiritual and cultural warfare has been ignored in the English speaking world, although, judging by the forthcoming economic collapse of the liberal System, it seems to be getting more and more attention.

Herfurth is a culture bearer in so far as he explains and interprets the ideas that have been crucial in shaping the behavior of modern political élites. Therefore his book will have a didactic value, especially for students in humanities who have been exposed for over half a century to "self- evident" truths of the liberal doctrine. But his book is also important insofar as he tirelessly demolishes the concepts that have been used by the communist and the liberal political class in an attempt to brainwash white peoples into pathological self-hate. The book could be aptly qualified as a manual of intellectual survival for a white novice entrapped in a jungle of politically correct, aesthetically correct and historically correct verbiage. It is a good travelling kit for all white nationalists interested in the power of ideas.

Herfurth's book carries a significant title, A Life in the Political Wilderness. One of his essays has the title "The Paris Hilton Syndrome," which is an allusion to, but also a real name of an American female celebrity whose real life stands for glitz, glamour and glory, but also for a hyper real image of a young liberalized Western woman in search of passing fame. The expression "Paris Hilton" has both real and surreal value. It is real insofar as it is represents a human being, albeit a vulgar female white trash; it is surreal insofar as the imagery of the title can be transposed into surreal ambiance of the real Hotel Hilton in Paris. Furthermore, the title can be also used metaphorically in the description of a syndrome of mimicry by white postmodern men and women who are willfully forfeiting their Self while projecting themselves into the Double, or better yet their better Other. Following the steps of great European thinkers, such as Julius Evola and Oswald Spengler (and a recently deceased postmodernist, Jean Baudrillard), Herfurth analyzes the contagious power of political simulacra in our postmodern media-conditioned society. The new role models are no longer muscled warriors such as Hector or Achilles, or Wolfhart and Giselher from the Germanic mythologies. The new hero today is an effeminate, bespectacled nerd, a castrate hermaphrodite, ruled over by a giant asexual bionic woman, sort of a Mega Diesel Dyke – and for good measure, a lurking Hollywood-engineered high IQ Afro-American scientist destined to act as a white man Superego, as a Doppelganger, as a cleanser of bad consciousness of the guilt -ridden white man. In the liberal vernacular ancient white heroes, or those who wish to emulate them, regardless of the epoch or the times they lived in, be they the antediluvian times or the modern times, must have an eternal stigma of "baaad Nazis." The dying liberal system, as Herfurth rightly remarks, resorts to the inversion of all values and interprets the role of the woman as just another perishable commodity; yet a commodity that dominates the man, fights the man, hates the man – and kills the man. In fact, our modern society, as can be observed in Herfurth's essays, has swept aside all of what our predecessors took for normal, healthy and attractive. Our gynaecocratic age (or why not call it a "vulvocratic age") has not liberated the white woman; it has created further rifts between women and men, killing all true femininity in the name of some abstract feminism. Western women are just simple toys in the merciless liberal System. Are they happier and "self-fulfilled" today? Nope. It suffices to take a look at the number of divorces in the USA, or the number of mistreated women in the so-called free world in order to grasp the verbal fraud of liberalism, known under the expression of "women's" liberation.

Herfurth defines well in his essays the root causes of our problem: the mendacity of the liberal System, the inversion of the meaning of the words, and the Reign of the Big Lie. "What is it exactly that makes our liberal democracies so good? Why are they preferable to these dictatorships and authoritarian regimes?" This is the question he raises and which liberal standard bearers do not like to hear. In the name of some purported interracial promiscuity and the glorification of different sexual life styles, the liberal System kills genuine diversity and authentic individualism – which have always been the foundation of White man's quest for liberty. Liberalism has imposed the most horrific type of herd- like consumerist conformism in which every critical thought is severely reprimanded. Of course, the liberal System allows every individual to work on his own "self expression" and "self-fulfillment," such as indulging in drugs, or sodomy, or the veneration of some Levantine freak or an Oriental, fakir or a guru; the System even encourages everybody to choose his own perversion and to tinker with zoophile or pedophilic escapades. But the minute a thoughtful white individual starts voicing doubts about the sacred canons of the liberal System, he is doomed. God forbid one should hazard into the liberal dogmas on multiculturalism, or tackle the liberal narrative about the World War II body counts! Herfurth does not talk from the top of his head. His native Germany loves bragging about being the freest country on Earth, yet it is also a country which does not hesitate a minute to fine or cart off to jail its heretics who committed the ultimate crime of asking questions that do not square away with the liberal mystique. So much for freedom of speech and diversity in liberalism.

The book has primarily an explanatory value as it clarifies concepts, words and their semantic deviations, a strategy which has been aptly applied by liberal propagandists. Herfurth draws attention to the fact that the modern masters of discourse have made words, such as "right vs. left" fit their own self-serving usage. Particularly in the German language the word right (Rechts) has acquired over the last 50 years a semi-criminal meaning – courtesy of liberal propaganda. In this aspect it may come as a surprise to a reader, particularly in Australia, that Herfurth uses in his essays the expression "The New Right" -- an expression with which he identifies as spokesman. Over and over again Herfurth explains that the label New Right and its original La Nouvelle Droite in France, does not stand for a political party or a movement wishing to scoop up votes for yet another parliamentary election. The New Right, with its scattered branches all over Europe and the USA stands basically for a loosely connected group of independent thinkers, writers and academics whose goal is to challenge the great myths of our time. The New Right is a cluster of courageous thinkers who delve into all pores of our post modernity and who dissect critically the communist-liberal Zeitgeist from esthetical, political and linguistic perspectives. Short of a better expression for now and given that we live in a world of passing etiquettes, labels and smears, there is no need to reject the label of the New Right, although time will tell which new label will be more appropriate in the future.

Although declaring himself as a member and founder of this cultural group, Herfurth's prose and message, under different socio-economic and historical circumstances, could easily pass off for leftist or anarchist writings! Or, simply put, heretic missives. The neurotic cleavage of right vs. left has caused immense misunderstandings amidst Whites over the last two hundred years. It needs to be abandoned urgently. Herfurth writes that by "doing that, we will appeal to a wider cross-section of the politically conscious community which is left-leaning, anti-globalist and anti-capitalist."

Herfurth discusses the burning issue of modern nationalism and how it can be framed in an appropriate fashion that would befit all Whites without pitting one against the other. Let us face it. The legacy of nationalism in Europe has been bad. Real bad. It has had a divisive and not a converging effect on all white European peoples. National identity, based on the hatred of one's mirror image in the neighboring White, needs to be rejected. Various manifestations of such negative nationalism are still strong in Europe, particularly in Eastern Europe. Such a nationalism functions only by the exclusion and resentment of neighboring nationalisms. Witness the tragedy of the artificial country of ex-Yugoslavia. Such mutually exclusive white nationalism only legitimizes the ongoing neo-Marxist and liberal experiment known as the ideology of multiculturalism.

Herfurth correctly argues that a new nationalism must first become a popular mass movement, particularly among young people. The best example is the German NPD, a party whose goal of strengthening the organic community among the youth should be used as a role model for other nationalist parties in Europe and the USA. "Nationalism has to be expressed as a style, as a way of life, before it can become an electoral movement." But the problem remains of how an American or an Australian nationalist can become receptive to that brand of nationalism considering the different historical frameworks in which their different nation-states were built. Many white nationalists, particularly in English speaking countries, wrongly assume that nationalism is just a matter of race, or of high IQ and of good white looks. Such an attitude is not just wrong but outright dangerous. Herfurth argues correctly that nationalism is primarily a cultural effort that necessitates first and foremost a strong spiritual reawakening rooted in a new definition of one's identity. In this sense modern young whites should actively engage in communal grass root activities that would blend them with their people. In the globalized world of today the concept of the nation- state has become redundant. The racial profile of the West, due to the mass non–European immigration, has changed the picture of Europe and America beyond recognition. Nobody should rule out that future white enclaves may emerge far away from the homes of their white ancestors, yet white enclaves able to sustain the cultural and racial memory of their white descendants.

Herfurth does not claim to be an "expert " or what the Germans call Fachidiot – a beautiful German word depicting a self-proclaimed savant obsessed with one single topic in his social analyses. The author does not harp on one single issue, such as the Jews, or the race, as many white nationalists do. His reflections go beyond simple black and white statements and ready- made formulas, so dear to liberal theoreticians in America. He is well aware that no matter what the outcome of the changing racial profile of America and Europe will be, neither him nor other white men in the West will be the only actors on the world stage.

Herfurth's last chapter deals with Tibet – a case study of a country and a people that has been subject to colonization by the Chinese government. And indeed, the case of Tibet is not just a story of an exotic Yeti, or a literary escapade of some levitating feel-good UN culinary diplomat, or the projection of leftist apostles bewailing the absence of human rights in China. It is more than that. It is a dramatic example of how peoples perish. And all whites can learn much from Tibetans.

"Now, we in the West are in the same boat as the Tibetans and Palestinians." In Herfurth's eyes Tibet is a judgment day scenario. Europe, similar to Tibet, has become a safe haven for non-white colonizers and judging by their number, Europe will soon turn into a raceless and mongrelized basket case with a few custom designed whites parading in special man made zoos. Modern liberal rulers, including their populace, are not fools; they are full of guilt feelings and afraid of halting the coming disaster. Yet, nobody among them wants to be tagged with a label of "racist" or "white supremacist," especially not the ruling class in Germany, Australia, or the USA. But their self-censorship will soon extol its price. And it will be very high. Their feigned humanism toward non-Europeans has nothing to with genuine respect for non-Europeans; it is a glaring sign of the lack of civic courage. And this is also a typical trait of many would-be nationalists in the West. Herfurth suggests that Whites need to become more proactive and avoid using insignia that compromises their struggle. There are ways they can establish a good sense of empathy, both with their foes and their friends. Even in view of the huge number of non-Europeans in the West, it does not mean that history has abruptly come to a stop. In fact, history has now entered into fifth gear, a sign that can only be detected by highly perceptive individuals. History has also shown us that a handful of committed individuals can literally change the face of the earth. History is open.

Obviously, all of us are aware that the issue of the future status of non-European immigrants in America, Europe and Australia needs to be addressed. Crafting wild scenarios about possible civil war and the break-up the West may not sound serious. But neither does the feigned optimism of the liberal ruling class sound serious. It is false to overestimate the political skills and the IQ of the liberal overclass, or rave about its conspiracy theories. However, when dominant ideas will have changed, so will the destiny of brainwashed people seriously change. Over 12 million German civilians were expelled from their homes in Eastern Europe in 1945 -- in a matter of weeks and with a shrug of shoulders by historians. Whether that gigantic expulsion was bad or good is beside the point. Probably Herfurth's parents could tell us that. It happened – and it did not augur the end of history. Mass expulsion or ethnic cleansing may happen again, albeit with different political actors and even in the opulence of Australia, the USA and Germany. If faced with the issue of their biological and cultural survival, who says that Whites in the USA or Australia cannot overhaul their own political behavior and redesign their destiny? Herfurth writes in his interesting book that "no one recognizes your rights unless you are prepared to fight for them."

I could only add that where there is a will there is always a way.

Tomislav Sunic
Zagreb
July 21, 2011

WELF HERFURTH: AGAINST THE REDUCTIO AD HITLERUM

His life

Francis Parker Yockey wrote, of his book Imperium, that the ideas in it were not original; but, in his defense, he declared that 'The craze for originality is a manifestation of decadence'. Certainly, Welf Herfurth is not an original: he is a standard-issue, 21st century German nationalist. But, outside of Germany, German nationalist ideas are little-known, or they are distorted by the mainstream liberal media. This is why Welf and his ideas appear, especially to Australians, so different and so compelling.

So who is Welf Herfurth? He is a German political activist, and businessman, who lives in Australia and who was born in West Germany in the 1960s. He is an interesting example of how the 'nationalist gene' skips one generation. Both of his grandfathers served in elite divisions of the Wehrmacht in the Second World War, and one of them was a member of the Sturmabteilung, who was expelled from the SA for marrying a German woman 'without permission'. His family suffered horribly, like millions of Germans, at the hands of the Allied victors after the war.

One would expect, then, that Welf's parents would be nationalists as well. But they are typical of the current generation of German 'baby-boomers': liberal democrats and fanatically anti-nationalist, praying to the god of money. The Germans of Welf's parents' generation are conditioned to react to German National Socialism, anti-Semitism, and racialism, with disgust and horror (and, in my experience, the Australians of my parents' generation are as well). The 'baby-boomers' in the West experienced a lot of brainwashing in the sixties and seventies; and part of the anti-nationalism of the German boomers is a revolt against one's parents, who were acquiescent at the time Hitler and his associates were busy gassing all those Jews and turning them into bars of soap, etc.

Welf became politically active as a young man. He spent some years in Iran with his family, when the revolution against the Shah broke out in 1979. He witnessed firsthand how oppressive governments can be overthrown and how America is running the internal politics of foreign countries, and, by doing so, how they try to establish the empire of the USA. Afterwards Welf did, and has continued to do, a great deal of travelling around the world - something which has enhanced his appreciation and respect for people of other races and cultures. It annoys Welf that so many nationalists think their country is the best and superior when they have never travelled.

Unfortunately, his life of activism, and his uncompromising nationalism, took its toll on his professional life: he lost three jobs in Germany because of his ideas, and eventually left for Australia in the 1980s. Once he arrived, he made contact with Dr. James Saleam, then of National Action, and joined, of all parties, the Australian Democrats - a left-liberal party, which, at the time, was an alternative party, and made it to the position of State Executive. The question is, why the Australian Democrats? The answer is that Welf was interested in the same social issues as the Democrats, and that the Democrats were the only genuine third party at the time.

Welf went on to join the Far Right populist party, One Nation, in the late 1990s, and became the vice-president for the state of New South Wales, directly under David Oldfield. Later, he founded the Sydney Forum, an annual conference for peoples of all political persuasions, with Dr Saleam. The Forum was born out of Inverell Forum, and was intended to break the barriers to left-right thinking, attract people of different political camps, and unite them on the issues that concern them.

Like a good many nationalists, Welf became disillusioned with One Nation, which self-destructed after its losses in the federal election of 1998 - in which it won a million votes, but not one seat. Welf felt, around this time, that he had taken party-political activism to the limit, and that it had so far gotten him nowhere. He now believed that the people who had become involved in One Nation were only interested in positions of money, power, and succeeding in the rat race. He began to look around for an alternative. He had long been interested in the ideas of Third Positionism and National Anarchism, and now began to apply them to his own activism, as we shall see below.

His politics

Welf is aged in his forties, but he has the appearance of someone who is ten years younger, as people who know him will attest. I think that Welf is, politically speaking, young as well. He has always seemed, to me, to be on the cutting edge of nationalist politics. I think that this is due to his remaining in contact with nationalist political movements in Germany, groups which have been forced to reinvent themselves constantly, and innovate, in the face of unrelenting political pressure. Welf himself likes to think outside of the square. He feels that his own thinking is different from that of many other nationalists, who tend to be racialist or anti-Semitic out of scape-goating - blaming others for their own failures.

A party like the NPD takes the 'long view' of nationalism. It has worked slowly to build up its political base, not going for a quick (but short-lived) electoral victory like the Front National or the British National Party. (Welf has little time for the far-right populist parties, and one of his favorite slogans is, 'a movement, not a party'). This makes the Germans different from the nationalist norm today.

Another pronounced difference is that the German nationalist scene, or certain sections of it (the NPD, the Free Nationalist/Free Comradeship/Autonomous Nationalist groups) are not Far Right in the conventional sense, and aim at taking politics beyond Left and Right. For that reason, the German nationalists will give someone like Hugo Chavez, for instance, a measure of support and which is why Welf is fond of reading biographies on Mao, Che Guevara and even Pol Pot. Like the German nationalists, Welf regards Guevara as something of a nationalist icon, and bought ten copies of Jon Lee Anderson's biography of Guevara and sent them to nationalists around Australia. Reading the book changed their views on Guevara, certainly, which is one of Welf's goals: to change people's political thinking and get them to think outside of what he calls 'the political cage'.

Welf could be said to be an importer of modern German nationalist ideas, and European ideas, to the Australian scene. He is always counseling Australian nationalist activists to use German organizational techniques, and to try to emulate some of the German propaganda (e.g., their use of left-wing slogans and symbolism, for example). For most of his time here in Australia, it is fair to say that his advice has fallen on deaf ears. It is only now that some activists are beginning to apply some of the 'German' methods and experiencing some success. In contrast to some other nationalists, Welf likes to step back from nationalism and consider what is wrong with it and how to fix it.

I think the breakthrough for Welf, politically, came with the founding of the New Right Australia blog and the accompanying website. He has always been interested in the ideas of Alain de Benoist and the Nouvelle Droite (and has met de Benoist). Troy Southgate, someone Welf greatly admires, held a New Right conference in London in 2005. This encouraged Welf to set up an informal organization, based roughly on the same principles as the Nouvelle Droit, in Australia - not a political party, but an intellectual and cultural movement. He launched two New Right Australia/New Zealand websites, and they have attracted attention from a good many nationalists around Australia, and even around the world. I think the reason for this success is the regular updating of content, and the quality of that content - deeply intellectual essays by Welf himself and other writers. The writing at New Right is intellectual, and at the same time, concerned with the day to day realities of nationalist political activism. It is that, combined with the freshness of its views, which makes New Right Australia/New Zealand unique. And it is through the medium of a popular, regularly-updated website that Welf has managed to get his ideas out (as well as through face to face contact and speeches at nationalist conferences).

Herfurthism?

Many people come up to Welf at nationalist conferences and ask, somewhat naively, if they can 'join' New Right. Welf will reply no, it's not a party. That impresses them, and gives them food for thought.

Welf is not against political parties per se. He believes in what the Germans call the 'three pillars strategy'. That is, nationalists must undertake a struggle to win control of the streets, win over the intellectuals, and win seats in the parliaments. In order to win the control of the streets, nationalists must have a constant, visible presence in the community, making themselves known through demonstrations, propaganda (such as pamphlets, posters, and the like) but also through community work and community activism. To a certain extent this entails social work - the 'soup kitchen strategy'. Welf points to the success of Hamas and Hezbollah in winning over large sections of the Palestinian and Lebanese people respectively. Hezbollah, for instance, is a religious group, a guerrilla army (which fended off the Israeli invasion of south Lebanon in 2006), an Islamic charity (responsible for, among other things, rebuilding bombed homes and providing food and support) and a political party. Welf very much approves of the tactics of the communist and fascist activists who, in Europe in the 1920s and the early 1930s, attempted to 'totalise' ordinary life - that is, build up parallel societies of all-fascist or all-communist schools, youth groups, hiking groups, trade unions, sports groups and the like. He is definitely an advocate of what Carl Schmitt called 'quantitative politics'. To Welf, most political parties are only interested in power of the party, not the people - the people are left behind and taken for granted by the party bureaucrats.

The point, I think, of the 'soup kitchen strategy' is threefold: firstly, it shows that nationalism is a social and a communitarian movement, addressing the neglected sectors of society; secondly, it works as propaganda, showing the public that, in contrast to the negative media image, nationalists are not so bad after all; third, it cements the hold of nationalism in the community. As stated before, Hamas and Hezbollah have succeeded in gaining support through such methods - and they are gaining more support than the other respective Palestinian and Lebanese parties, who have restricted their activism to campaigning in elections. Having said that, the 'soup kitchen strategy' goes beyond mere charity work: it can include participation in the SES (the Australian State Emergency Service), the Red Cross, the local fire brigade...

And it is this emphasis on community activism which merges with another part of the 'Herfurth doctrine'. Welf, so long as I have known him, has always believed in the importance of networking and face to face contacts. He is prepared to talk, and have associations with, any nationalist who has an open mind. He, for instance, maintains a relationship with the skinheads of Blood and Honor. Skinheads are not an always well-regarded section of the nationalist movement, but Welf shrugs off any criticism. One of Welf's rules of thumb is not to believe in what the media says about certain groups, and to keep an open mind. He is always prepared to attend the meetings of the Australian Greens, or Resistance (an Australian communist group), or the conservative Sydney Institute, or even any mainstream liberal democratic party.

As well as that, Welf thinks that face-to-face contact is necessary for creating a positive impression. The Internet has proven to be a boon to nationalism, but at the same time, it has the tendency to breed isolation, and with it, rumor-mongering. This is one of the reasons why many nationalists in Australia cannot maintain a working relationship and undertake mass activism: they have not met one another in person and tend to believe negative rumors about x activist spread on the Internet. It is face-to-face contact, in Welf's view, which removes the barriers of distrust and isolation, and dispels negative rumors. This is one of the reasons why he recommends the German 'Freie Nationalist' organizational techniques. He understands that the Internet, combined with rumors and gossip, can lead to others developing a false perception of himself - which is why he thinks personal contact with him will help change that false perception.

Another part of Welf's world view is what I consider to be left-wing radicalism. This may be surprising to a few, even in nationalism, who are used to viewing nationalism in the West as being 'Extreme Right' or 'Far Right'. (And, indeed, the liberal democratic politicians, media and academia classify nationalism as such). Without a doubt, there are many conservatives, politically on the Right, in the nationalist movement - particularly in the populist parties. But I would call the NPD a left-wing party, and Mahler, for one, has no problems in reconciling the ideals of the NPD and modern German nationalism with those of the radical German student movement of the late 1960s (and the Red Army Faction). And it is a radical left-wing view which informs Welf's thinking - in its opposition to capitalism, globalization, American imperialism, consumer culture, liberal democracy and liberal individualism. Welf has a fondness for anarchist-type slogans ('Smash the system') and, as noted before, takes great inspiration from the heroes of the conventional extreme Left. He thinks that the Left has succeeded in convincing the public that it, the Left, has a monopoly on certain issues (like the environment); the political system works on polarizing people and splitting them into separate groups (in the way that the US media, for instance, classifies everyone as either 'liberal' or 'conservative').

There is more to Leftism, and socialism, than a few anti-capitalist slogans - but an attempt to reach a definition of 'leftism' and 'socialism' would be beyond the scope of this article. But part of the problem with seeing the likes of the NPD and the Freie Nationalisten as being on the Left, politically, is that communism, in the 20th century, successfully hijacked the term, and manage to convince a good part of the world that anything non-Marxist and non-communist is not truly 'left-wing' at all. (And that includes socialist movements with a large working-class following: for instance, Fabian socialism). Liberal socialist parties like the British Labor Party, or the Australian Labor Party, are not left-wing, in the Marxist view. Juan Peron, Huey Long, Gamal Nasser, are not left-wing, and not socialist, because they were not communist (and Peron and Nasser actively persecuted communists in their respective countries). As for Benito Mussolini and Adolf Hitler, they were reactionary tools of capitalism - men who used socialist-sounding slogans and ideas to lure people away from the one true socialism, Marxism.

Communism's rigid adherence to the Marxist dogmas, and its refusal to accept the existence of alternative forms of leftism and socialism, was one of the reasons for its success in the 20th century. But in the 21st century, it has been left floundering. Its inability to adapt to changing social conditions - indeed, Marxism is a theory that the future development of humanity has been worked out in a few books written 150 years ago - has meant that non-Marxist socialists like Hugo Chavez and Subcomandante Marcos have taken centre stage. (Chavez calls his project 'Socialism for the 21st century'). A big hole exists in the West, left by the implosion of Marxism and the decline of mainstream social democracy, which can be filled by nationalism. The German nationalists, and Welf, understand this perfectly, and attempt to persuade other nationalists that phenomena such as immigration are due to globalization and neoliberalism. The modern Left is often too slow to change its thinking when it comes to these issues, because they have degenerated into personality cults (the cult of Marx, Lenin, Mao, Castro, whoever) and cannot think beyond the labels they apply to all and sundry.

Welf often laments that nationalists, in Australia at least, fail to grasp how causes championed by communists, anarchists, mainstream liberals and social democrats, can be exploited by nationalism. He recently told me of a nationalist conference where David Hicks was denounced as a traitor and an Islamist, whereas he would have liked to have undertaken activism on behalf of Hicks. The same US military tribunals used to 'prosecute' Hicks were used to 'prosecute' German soldiers at Nuremberg (especially in the second set of Nuremberg trials). Many nationalists, however, fail to see the connection. (It is not that Welf believes in what Hicks believes in; merely that he feels the politicians have sacrificed Hicks in order to further their own political interests).

Finally, Welf is one of the most tolerant nationalists I have come across. He has travelled widely, having gone to over fifty countries, and respects all ethnic groups - in their own lands. He thinks that most nationalist propaganda today is too negative, aiming at demeaning other races and spreading 'hate' (his word), instead of trying to make a case for all the good things nationalism can do for one's community.

In conclusion

Welf has a great dislike of what he calls 'labels'. Because he is German, and a nationalist, he is often called (even by other nationalists in Australia) a 'Neo-Nazi'. Welf is, of course, a German patriot, and naturally is an enthusiastic supporter of Germany's cause in the Second World War (and every other war before that). He has a few mild criticisms of German National Socialism, but in the main supports it as one phase in the development of German nationalism. He is baffled by the phenomenon of 'Nutzism' - that is, Americans and other non-Germans who claim to be "National Socialist" and who dress in home-made Sturmbabteilung and Schutz Staffel uniforms, and has even encountered a few in Australia. To Welf, the term 'Neo-Nazi' refers to these people, and no other. So he is somewhat irritated when people apply the label to him. (Certain opponents of nationalism apply the term to everyone, regardless of their beliefs. I always find it amusing when someone, inappropriately, applies the term 'Neo-Nazi' to me or one of my nationalist friends. Welf, however, does not).

Germany, these days, cannot be patriotic, because the entire world - and the German establishment itself - focuses on one tiny portion of Germany history (the period from 1933 to 1945). Sixty years on, Hollywood and the Western mass media are still waging war on Germany (where would Hollywood be without German National Socialism?). In this regard, Welf found a new book called 'The Hitler

Club', by Gary Gumpl and Richard Kleinig (describing the wartime persecution of German-Australians by the Australian government) relevant:

The Australian authorities and press were happy to peddle the fallacy which Leo Strauss (the German-born Jewish philosopher and ethicist who had studied under Martin Heidegger and is regarded as one of the intellectual pillars of the American Neoconservative movement) in 1950 called the reductio ad Hitlerum. It was also facetiously called the argumentum ad Nazium. This fallacy, said Strauss, took the form that, if Hitler or the Nazi Party supported a policy or course of action, then such policy or action must necessarily be evil. Becker was unwittingly and inextricably caught up in its clutches. ('The Hitler Club', p. 389).

I value Welf for the great energy and devotion that he brings to his struggle - a struggle which, in part, I identify with, and hundreds of thousands of European nationalists identify with. Welf is someone who gets things done; he is also someone possessed of a fanatical sense of loyalty to his people. If we had thousands more men like Welf, working as political activists, the national revolution, not only in Germany, but all across the West, would be soon at hand. And that, despite the fearful prognostications of Jews, communists and liberals, would be a good thing and not a bad thing. It is through Welf that I have come to know the decency of the German people, and German nationalism, and, by extension, nationalists in the West. Others, through Welf, will come to know it too.

Tim Johnstone

FOREWORD

One of the most common questions I am asked is why I am so interested and passionate about politics, especially nationalistic politics. And my answer is always the same; it is not only an interest but a duty to my nation and to my people. You see, we are all living together in our families, our communities and nations, on this fantastic planet and who else but we, the people, can and will look after our well-being and the future of our children and their children to come.

My passion for this has lead me to being called a Nazi, Fascist, Communist, Race traitor and many more labels, mainly because people do not understand what I am about and what my goals are. And many people do not want to understand what I am all about, or any other person or ideology they do not agree with, because they are living in a political and social cage, afraid of expanding their horizon.

One of the most interesting experiences I had was when a young man told me about this bad person, a dangerous Nazi, and after I talked with him for about an hour and we found we agreed on almost everything. This young man was a member of a so called left wing organization and a self confessed Antifascist. The person he was telling me about was actually me. When I told him that he was talking about me the look on his face was priceless. Here we were agreeing with most of the issues we have just talked about and now it turned out that I am not what he believed in. Guess what, he just walked away…….. Never to been seen or heard of again.

I have been interested in politics since I was a young boy growing up in a wonderful small town in Germany. While I was playing in the forest and busy damming up little creeks and catching fish, the German Red Army Faction (RAF) killed people, the Italian Brigate Rosse was blowing up bombs and the Irish Republican Army caused havoc not only in Ireland and England, but all over Europe. Together they managed to turn Europe into a state of emergency. Street blockades with police armed with submachine guns, passport controls and daily terror alerts in the news were common and went on for years.

When my family moved to Iran, I witnessed the revolution first hand and I realized how swiftly a government can be overturned if the people have the will to do so. Now the Shah's secret police and the army was nothing to be taken lightly, equipped with the latest US army hardware, they were an impressive sight. Seeing tanks on every street corner with soldiers armed to the teeth should stop any crowd. However, the Iranian people were just sick of the regime's oppressive rule and the ever increasing American influence and had nothing to lose. So the revolution took its turn......

Returning to Germany in 1979, I was confronted with large demonstrations of German people in support of the political struggle in Nicaragua, El Salvador, etc. Nothing wrong with that, but where was the outcry and demonstrations in support of our own people who lived just across the border in East Germany? When I asked people about this, I was told that we as Germans have to live with it forever as a punishment for the atrocities of the Third Reich.

I went to my first political meeting in 1979, attending a rally of the NPD, There I was asked to hold up a banner that demanded German reunification. We were only a handful of people that were there to listen to the speaker. But literally hundreds of people were demonstrating against the NPD, using whistles to drown out the speaker and throwing eggs and other objects at us.

And we were called Nazis, something I had no idea what this was. So I informed myself about what a so called Nazi is and I came to the conclusion that a Nazi is something that existed between 1919 and 1945 and died with the fall of the Third Reich.

I was very active in the NPD and met numerous interesting people, from former SS soldiers, to political con men and fanatical nationalists and national socialists. And while I did not always agree with them I always spoke with them and let them tell me what they believed in. After all we were living in a so called democracy that encouraged political and social discussions and different opinions. And I learned a great deal from these people, even if it was about what not to do....

In 1982 I went to South America and while traveling this wonderful continent I realized the enormous impact of US politics and the imperialistic expansion not only of American policies, but American companies. It was sad to see that whole governments in South America are ruled not by the native people, but by some people in boardrooms in the US. The corruption and brute force that was unleashed by these people was frightening and destroyed more than one culture, all in the name of globalization and profit.

Now until this point I was a great supporter of America as they protected the good West from the evil empire in the East. America and Capitalism were our protectors that gave us McDonald's and Coca Cola. The Russians and their Communism were the evil beasts that would destroy us all. We grew up and we didn't know better as the governments and the systems made sure that we heard and learned only what they wanted us to know.

After the trip to South America it was clear to me that the youth in the western world were as brain washed as the people under the rule of Russia. But the difference was that in the West the method of brain washing was to turn us into mindless consumers that do not question the liberal democratic system.

Conform and consume.

In 1986 I went on a year long trip around the world that ended with me settling permanently in Australia. During that trip I saw countries like Mongolia, China and the whole of South East Asia. It was an absolute once in a lifetime experience; seeing the countries and their cultures, speaking to the locals and living with them was something that taught me the value of different cultures and how important it is to preserve this for future generations. After all, who in the future wants to see the Lao culture in a Lao style Disneyland?

In Australia I continued my political activism as I saw it as my responsibility to be active in the communities I live in. I dabbled in the libertarian politics of the Australian Democrats where, again, I meet very good people that seriously wanted to change the government and social life. What struck me was the willingness of them to open all borders to all the refugees and let everybody enter Australia in the name of compassion. That is compassion for everybody else but ultimately not for Australians.

In the middle of 1990 Pauline Hanson was elected to the Australian federal parliament and caused a storm with her maiden speech, demanding a stop to immigration and more rights for Australians. She was immediately labeled a racist, Nazi, etc and her public events were demonstrated against. The media, which made her in the first place, turned on her and a public witch-hunt was conducted. The Jewish News even published a list with all the names and addresses of One Nation members.

One of the most disturbing things I learned in my time in One Nation was the absolute belief of most of the members in the political system and civic nationalism. Populism was rampant and Australia was, and still is, the BEST country in the world in their mind. When I asked people if they had ever been outside the country, most of them looked at me with a blank stare and asked me why they should leave the country as it is the best in the world. Now call me naïve, but how can one say that something is the best if they have never experienced anything else? How can somebody support a system that is repressing their own people and the people want to keep what is destroying them?

One Nation died a slow death and Pauline Hanson went on to stand for several elections, always polling well and pocketing some handsome election fund returns.

Around 1999 I started to ask myself the question of what I am doing with my political life and what I am really trying to achieve. For nearly 20 years I tried to change politics for the better, giving the people more say in their life and the running of their country. And I realized that the liberal democratic systems in the western world do everything and anything to stop people like me as they do not want to give up their power and influence. Understandably, I have to admit; why would they give up their place in the system.

I also questioned my ability to change big political issues, like globalization, immigration, survival of whole cultures, stopping the impact of imperialism, etc. Here I was having just witnessed the total destruction of the One Nation Party, a party that had been voted for by nearly 1 Million people, nearly 10% of the total vote, and all the time and money of the members was for nothing.

Around this time I started a correspondence with Troy Southgate and heard about National Anarchism. The first time I read the term National Anarchist I thought it was an oxymoron. Isn't Anarchism the complete opposite to Nationalism? But after reading what National Anarchism is all about it became all so clear to me what it is and I embraced it like a long lost friend.

And the rest is history.

Now, dear reader, why do I tell you all this and give you my life story? The answer is very simple – we all have to find our path in life and learn from our experiences.

I am the first one to admit that we are all different. The propaganda of the liberal democratic press that we are all equal is Bulldust. We all, and I mean all the people on this planet, have different experiences, cultures and identities. That is what makes us individuals and human beings. That is why we have different beliefs and political and social expectations.

And the system knows that and exploits it to create divisions between people. Right, Left, Libertarian and all the other labels the media sticks on political activists is nothing but to divide people. Who after all wants to talk to a Nazi, a Communist, a Greenie, etc? Who wants to go hang out with Skinheads, Hippies, Communists, etc.?

If there is something that I absolutely agree with and practice it is that I have no fear of association. I am more than happy to have a political dialogue with people from the so called left, right or whatever they are labeled or whatever they label themselves. For me there is no political boundary as we are all people that have an opinion and some of us are even courageous enough to stand up for those opinions.

The writings in this book are a reflection of my opinions and my thoughts. People helped me in putting them to paper as English is not my first language and I am forever grateful for their help. You might not agree with some of the statements and opinions and I am glad about this as I don't want people reading this and agreeing 100%. If this is the case, think about what you really believe in and what you want.

Personally I am happier than ever. I am still politically active, running a small book service that helps people to educate themselves. I meet interesting people, address different political and social meetings and I am active in a volunteer fire brigade. I am connected with the community I live in, have great friends and live how I want to live – connected, involved, and active. I do what I can do to change things on a level that I have influence in and can change. Having said that I still support the political parties that stand up against the system and the danger of globalization and I wish them well.

Last, I want to thank you for reading this book. Not because I make money from it as I promise you that is not the case. But because you show me that there are still people out there who are free thinkers and who refuse to give up the fight for a better world for all the people who live on it and future generations.

Think Globally – Act Locally and destroy what destroys you.

Welf Herfurth
Sydney, July 2011

1

DISCUSSING RACE IN A GLOBAL WORLD

The subject of race and racial difference is something a lot of people avoid. Some consider it bad manners or impolite. Others say it is offensive and discussion of it should be suppressed by legislation. One spin-off from that category goes as far as to deny the existence of races, claiming any number of religious, philosophical, scientific (sic) and moral theories in support of the proposition. Then, some fellow travelers might conclude that races exist in some narrow, almost meaningless sort of way and may conclude that, for 'human-universalist' reasons - they should be abolished.

Of course, there are people - amongst all races - who believe their particular origin renders them wise or good or superior. The fact this class of human beings exists might condition the attitudes of those who prefer the matter not bedevil us further. Sometimes this group is downright offensive and some amongst them have a genocidalist frame of mind. However, that does not make the existence of races as such invalid. The old Chinese who spoke of others as barbarian or the Hitlerite who took refuge in false aesthetics or the Zionist Jew who believes some peoples are lesser entities are used as an excuse by many to refuse to entertain any theory of race that proclaims a virtue in their existence.

I am not afraid to discuss race. Because I am prepared to accept races exist, I must therefore say: "Where did they come from? What does it mean?"

I see race and species as different. I certainly agree that humans, as a whole are a species, but within the family you have different races. It is like in the animal world. You have dogs, cats, whales, deer, etc., but within each 'species' you have different 'races'. It might be a simplistic description, but take the species of dogs. You have your German Shepherd, Schnauzer, Fox Terrier, etc. They are all dogs, but they are different - in looks, size and temperament. They can interbreed, if you really want to, but the sense of individuality might ultimately be lost. In my opinion that is the same with humans. We all walk on two legs; have a head and arms and legs. We think, have needs and we need to love and be loved. We communicate with each other and we have always regarded ourselves as related to each other. There is no doubt that we are, however, very special 'animals' (I note there may be certain religious opposition to this label being applied, but my purpose should quickly become clear). Essentially, we have self-awareness. The philosophers have long debated that notion. It is the capacity to think in 'higher' terms, moral terms, to distinguish wants and needs, to regulate impulse, to act socially, that makes the human species special. Why should we be surprised if nature has equipped each of the races slightly differently?

Between the different races we note great differences. Not only the skin color, but also how we act in different situations and our physical abilities. The Negroid race is generally a more physical race than the Asian or 'Indian' or European or Semite. He has the well known (if always given in cliché form) abilities at certain sports and song, of physical labor and in the endurance of pain. Some Asian groups on the other hand have a higher IQ than the white man, and a capacity for skilled application to the finery of life and culture. The Eskimo have a high IQ, but black groups seem to come in at the bottom of the range. Then the white man is generally more practical and scientific. The Semitic groups have the ability to form intricate systems of religious and mystical Gnostic thought. In some ways, each is 'better' than another and in some ways 'lesser'.

There are also differences within the races whereby each may be broken into sub-groups. We just have to look at the Europeans. They are 'white', but the Italians are different to the Swedish, the Germans are different culturally and temperamentally to the Russians. But this difference is mainly based on their habits, which is influenced by the culture they live in. There are also certain anatomical variations. I suppose we could apply that principle to the Asian race. Japanese are 'fairer' to Vietnamese; Han Chinese have heavier frames to Thais. The skull of the Ethiopian may be easily compared to the Senegalese and the legendary collectivity of the Zulu contrasts with the freer structures of Sierra Leone. And so forth.

This incredible difference between races and variation within races is a natural thing. We can say God made it that way (if we are religious in our view) or we can say nature made it that way (if we are evolutionists). Whichever way, we are dealing with a fact of existence. It seems to be a wondrous fact. The differences in humanity cannot be a thing decried, but only accepted. Once accepted, we should celebrate it. If one is religious in outlook we could say that if it was made that way, it is not to be tampered with. If we are scientific in our outlook, we would say that nature's processes are not to be willed away. I would venture to say that a proper discussion of the existence of race implies a revolution in philosophy against political correctness.

When I do my travels, I always love to cross a border and be instantly in a different world. Just going from Germany to Switzerland is amazing. The landscape might be the same as might be the architecture, but the people and the cultures are different. And that is what I would like to preserve. Look at Europe today. You have so many other races living in England that more than half of London is non-white. If we go to some countries in the Arab world, we would think we were in Pakistan. If we go to India, we find people wanting to be Americans and chatting away only in English. What effect does all this pseudo-globalization have on the economy of this country? What about the survival of the heritages of the 'native' peoples? I am German, but I would not be offended if people in an African country became annoyed with too many of our tourists or businessmen making pests of themselves. It does not offend me as a 'white man' to learn Malaysians painted large slogans back in the 1950's: "British go home!", "White Man: Pack Up Your Burden". It is always 'numbers' and 'weight' that drives a people to demand a bit of living room. I wasn't upset either when Libya sent home many of its guest workers or when Nigeria packed off its illegal immigrants. Nor am I offended when an Icelander asks the question why do they need Indians in their country? It almost seems that if everyone was in his 'place', being himself, there would be less tension and more respect?

Where does all the pressure for 'one world' end? Let us imagine every person on this planet became chocolate colored with dark hair and dark eyes. No more Asian, African, European or Indian races. Let us assume, therefore, that there was no more racial diversity in people. Let us assume we could teach one language, use one money-system, knock down all barriers and borders and live in one huge market place. Where would the benefit be? Do we really think that that in itself would make for a better mankind or a more harmonious or prosperous or culturally achieving world? And of course, can we assume that if we could put humanity through a blending machine that differentiation might not reappear, in a new form perhaps, but still operate in human affairs?

Of course what is different often has the appeal of the exotic and one cannot prevent the small scale mixing of the races. In certain places too at different times this has occurred on a visible scale, with historical and cultural forces operating to produce new results over long periods. But when we are confronted by those who suggest it should be the norm and be pursued consciously and aggressively, then we must act to prevent the large-scale destruction of singular identities and struggle hard to preserve the diversity of humanity.

I do not know if there is an agenda to encourage the one-world result. It could be the naivety or foolishness or greed of people who push this vision. However, I have come to think there is a push from Western liberals, capitalists of all colors, some theologians and others to create 'one-world'. World-improvers of all sorts and the so-called liberals are promoting the idea that diversity is a tiresome nothing. There can be no doubt that these delightful sounding platitudes will serve those who see that by breaking down all boundaries, humanity is better 'managed' in a market-millennium. For one, I would attack that sort of 'vision' as a monstrosity and prefer the racial differences and diversity. And I would argue that we are not "naturally gravitating" towards The Great Brown Race, but we are being in fact resettled.

I know that in today's western society discussing the race issue is rather sticky and a dangerous ground to walk on. But I am willing to do that. I believe that the survival of the different races and cultures is as important as the survival of the whale, elephants and different birds. It is a worthy goal if it is kept as a celebration of diversity as essential to overall human progress. We are still a family.

To keep to such a goal, I would repudiate any notion that one race is better than another race in a hierarchy arranged from the best to the least. It is precisely because the races have different skills and aptitudes and possibly deficits that this cannot be done. I am left to say that the races are equal - but they are not the same. We can and we should accept that these differences are recorded in our cultures. Our cultures are the windows to our souls. They define each of the races, each of the sub-types, each of the peoples. These cultures are treasures. They can be appreciated by each of the human types, but they are only fully lived and appreciated only by their creator group. Surely a race or a nation has the right to retain their nation's culture and identity in their own country. Where is the arrogant self-assertion in that? If a race or other group owns a culture, it has the right to prefer to retain it.

Could we have a world of peoples in definable zones as an alternative to the New World Order of chaos and destruction? Perhaps that is the ultimate expression of the argument I am putting here! But the agenda of the political liberals, the mass media outlets and the entertainment industry in promoting multiculturalism (which in my opinion is actually liberal monoculture) in Western societies will, in effect, destroy the European cultures. However, their model is now increasingly pushed upon other peoples as part of New World Order imperialism. It is a strange imperialism that comes to divest the conquered of their culture and then to merge its wreckage with the wreckage of others. I am pleased to note many people are rising against this model.

I always liked travelling and seeing the world. It gives me the feeling of being alive and interacting with people and place. I will never understand how people can live in one place and one place only - and think that they are living in "the best place" on earth. Each land may be a great country, but there is no such thing as "the best place". Similarly we can discard the idea of the best race. In a world that seems to be losing its way and descending into conflict, we should seek the causes. They do not only lie in the rivalries of races, nor has this sort of rivalry brought the human world to the brink of destruction. If we look back into history, it certainly involved conflicts of races and peoples and evil deeds. However, the past also possessed an outline principle of diversity as being essential to progress overall. Whatever the differences were and the contentions they produced, there was amongst all the idea of a certain security in the arrangements. This is now challenged by the false anti-racism of one-world-ism.

Let us discuss race. Let us see whether the defense of race offers a challenge to one-world-ism. That is a good place to start. If we like the fruits of this discussion, we can take it further. It may be the revolutionary idea to put up against same-ness, conformity, the drab, the destructive and globalization.

We are all equal, but we are not the same

2

THE PROS AND CONS OF THE NOUVELLE DROITE

I

Recently, the New Right Australia-New Zealand blog[1] published a lengthy criticism of Alain de Benoist's ideas by Michael O'Meara. I thought it would be opportune to write a similar piece, one which will look at the possibility of applying de Benoist's ideas to the Australian nationalist scene and the wider political spectrum in general.

Anyone who has read de Benoist books and articles will know that one of the advantages of de Benoist's work is that it is purely social political. That is, it is political philosophy - it discusses the State and how it works, or how it should work. It is not restricted to rants against Jews, Muslims and Negroes, or other immigrant groups foreign to the Western societies. This is a refreshing change - to read a nationalist who is an intellectual first and foremost, like Evola or Yockey, and who is not simply some person writing emotive diatribes against people of foreign races.

At the centre of de Benoist's work lies the concept of the organic community. By 'organic community', I mean a community that has sprung up naturally, and developed over a long period of time, with a natural degree of cohesiveness. Each of the members feel a sense of belonging to an organic community, and the community does not contain elements that are radically different from it. The majority of the Western countries, before the mass immigration explosion of the 1970s and 1980s, could be considered organic in this sense (even if their official ideologies were liberal and hence individualist). It is this 'organicism' which has drawn accusations of racism from de Benoist's opponents, although an organic community may not be necessarily based on race - one has to think of Islam, for example (the Muslims consider themselves first and foremost Muslims in a religious sense and racial differences are overlooked as long as they are Muslims).

---

[1] http://newrightausnz.blogspot.com

De Benoist's politics owes a great deal to Evola (at least in his later work), who writes at length on empire and how subject peoples exist in an autonomous relationship to the centre of an empire. The Austro-Hungarian Empire, for instance, consisted of a large number of ethnically homogenous, independent communities (including the Serbs, Czechs, Slovenes, et al.) which maintained a sense of identity and separateness despite their being the subjects of the same empire. The parts existed independently of the whole. That system - which could be described as a system of ethnic federalism - is one that de Benoist regards as ideal.

The danger to any ethnic federalism comes from two ideologies. The first is nationalism: paradoxically, de Benoist is anti-nationalist in the traditional Far Right sense. The First World War broke out when one ethnic group - the Serbs – demanded that their community constitute itself as a nation, with a sovereign state, flag, currency, army, and everything that belongs to an independent country, and the right to ethnically purge citizens from that nation's territory. The collapse of the Empire, and Woodrow Wilson's insistence on granting nationhood to those ethnic groups, hastened the swing towards nationalism in Eastern and Central Europe and the destruction of a traditionalist order.

The second danger is multiculturalism. Again, the example of South-Eastern Europe applies. After the Second World War, the various ethnic groups that made up part of the Austrian-Hungarian Empire were forcibly amalgamated into an artificial entity called Yugoslavia by the communist Tito. Anyone who continued to identify themselves as Serb, Croat, Slovene, et al., was shot. And this is typical: the feeling of belonging to a long-established, organic community is so strong that only totalitarian violence can repress it. Ethnic structures and their identity are suppressed and destroyed by the might of the gun, with brutal force and/or with unnatural laws.

Again, this is one of the themes of Evola's work. Totalitarianism is the natural outcome of the decline of empires (a good example is the French revolution and the rise of Napoleon). Under totalitarianism, the parts of the whole can no longer exist in an autonomous relationship to the center, the government. Instead, the government must impose itself, by force, upon the parts. Bureaucracy and repression crushes any individuality, and wipes out any autonomy. Along the way, distinguishing characteristics of ethnic groups are removed. Everyone becomes like everyone else, and organic communities are artificially merged into one, giant inorganic and artificial community.

II

Much of this applies to the Australian case. Non-white immigrants, upon arriving in Australia, are told that they must renounce their identity - whether it be Arab, Turks, Vietnamese, Chinese or lately the Sudanese– and 'become Australian'. This sense of 'Australianism' is rather artificial: it is certainly not based on race. The 'old' Australia, before multiculturalism and unrestricted non-white immigration, was Anglo-Saxon and Anglo-Celt in terms of its ethnicity. Even the immigrants from Europe, especially Eastern and Southern Europe, who came here after the Second World War, did not alter this. But now anyone can become Australian - all one needs is an Australian passport. Australians today are defined by a piece of paper that states what they are and not by ethnicity, culture or race.

The same applies, too, in Britain, where the official State ideology is that Indians and colored immigrants are 'British' (even though they and their descendants only arrived thirty years ago) as Shakespeare and Dickens. In Germany, Germans are told to consider the Turkish communities as German as Schiller, Goethe and Bach. And if any organization or political party like the National Democratic Party of Germany (NPD) refused to accept them as Germans and argue against their inclusion as Germans, they are labeled as racists, Neo-Nazis and misguided haters.

Paradoxically, however, the immigrant groups in the West refuse to 'assimilate', i.e., renounce their cultural heritage and ethnic origins. One only has to take a walk through the Vietnamese or Chinese diaspora communities in Sydney or Melbourne to see that that process of 'Australianisation' is not occurring. These communities stubbornly cling to their sense of identity; they mostly live in their own ghettoes, visit their own restaurants and shops and pray in their own churches or mosques.

And indeed, Vietnam has a great history, as does China. Both were, in their respective distant pasts, traditionalist societies. Australia, on the other hand, has never been traditionalist: it is a product of liberalism, capitalism and British colonialism. So why would anyone want to become 'Australian' and forgo being Vietnamese or Chinese? Why trade your traditional values in and assimilate for being a "Paper Australian"?

But multiculturalism is as much a danger to the immigrant communities as it is to their host populations, as the Muslims in Australia are finding out. Multiculturalism insists that peoples assimilate to an artificial, inorganic type of community. Hence the State campaign in Australia to 'educate' Muslims in 'Australian values', i.e., pro-multiculturalist, and pro-Israel, values.

III

If one takes a nationalist approach in de Benoist's sense, one will say that Australia is a nation and that that nationhood is based, on the whole, on race, and that anyone not belonging to the Anglo-Celtic or European races should be purged. It may be desirable, to someone of this ideology, for a Balkanisation of Australia to take place, where some parts of Australia which are ethnically homogenous and white cede from the parts that are not, and purge themselves of non-white elements.

Organizations and certain individuals on the Far Right tend to speculate that a scenario like the latter will occur and dream about the coming 'Race War'. Many of them (including the fans of The Turner Diaries) want to bring it on. And when in December 2005 the people in Cronulla stood up against the Lebanese gangs that terrorized 'their shire' the hopes of a full blown 'Race War' was high in certain groups like the web based forum "Stormfront".

And, of course, nationalists in other parts of the Western world envisage the same scenario for their own countries. De Benoist's ideas, which are opposed to this sort of nationalism, may not appeal to too many on the Far Right.

It must be admitted that de Benoist can be accused of shilly-shallying on the immigrant question. In contrast, Guillaume Faye seems to take the standard view. The Faye position, so far as I can discern, is that the North African and Arab communities in France must be expelled and repatriated, or segregated.

Benoist, on the other hand, has no clear cut solution to offer. He, of course, regards the immigrant presence as a blight and a burden, calling immigration a 'disaster'. He recognizes that the immigrants are as badly off under the existing multicultural arrangement as the host population. But he seems to think that nothing can be done, or should be done.

Faye's position has the advantage of clarity and firmness - qualities that will always appeal to the Far Right. He names the enemy (Islam), concentrates all his resources on one single enemy, and attacks. He is a philo-Semite, or at least, prefers not to acknowledge the role that the Zionists - and the ideology of the Holocaust - have played in spreading the virus of multiculturalism throughout the West. But he is not evasive like De Benoist, who counsels 'realism' in the face of the immigrant problem, which some may say is a formula for inaction.

What would be a solution which is in keeping with de Benoist's ideas? The answer is, I think, ethnic federalism, or at least the spirit of ethnic federalism. Governments in the West should give the diaspora communities of Asians, Muslims, Black, Indians, Kurds, Turks and others more autonomy, more freedom. They should be given more political power, and not have power taken away from them (which is what the white nationalist, bent on Turner Diaries-style ethnic cleansing, seeks to do). The immigrant communities tend to be self-segregating anyway. It is merely a matter, then, of granting them sovereignty and jurisdiction to make them fully independent. By that means, the system of the Austrian-Hungarian Empire can be recreated on our doorstep.

Now before I will get a barrage of e-mails from people accusing me of giving up Australia as we know it, or want to remember it, I certainly don't agree fully with this solution. This is just one possible application of de Benoist ideologies and ideas.

IV

Something that is unique in de Benoist's theory is his approach to democracy. To De Benoist, democracy is to be defined as the participation of the community in the running of its own affairs. (He means, of course, organic communities).

Unlike thinkers such as Evola and Yockey, de Benoist places a high value on democracy. One of his theses is that democracy is compatible with Traditionalism – that parliaments have existed, in one form or another, in traditionalist societies like, for example, in the old Greek or Roman empires. One of the drawbacks of modern liberal democracy is, so de Benoist claims, that it is not democratic enough. That is, it does not allow the community to order and rule its own life but is ruled by a political and business elite. Multiculturalism insists on amalgamating organic communities into inorganic and artificial ones, therefore denying them any meaningful democracy.

De Benoist views freedom as being something more or less the same thing as democracy. Following Aristotle, he defines freedom as the capacity to participate in one's cultural life, in the life of one's community. By participating in the day to day business of the organic community, one transcends one's own individualism - the sphere of one's private life. To de Benoist, the individual's private life, his means of making a living and the rest, is the sphere of necessity. It is only one's actions in the sphere of one's ethnic group, one's race and community that can be said to be free.

De Benoist, naturally enough, has some sympathy for communitarianism. The mainstream of communitarian thought, however, is not nationalist (in the sense of belonging to the traditional Far Right). De Benoist's ideas could be described, then, as 'nationalist' (in our sense) communitarianism.

Such a political philosophy is much more positive than the standard white nationalism/Nutzism/Far Right nationalism, which is geared towards kicking the Negroes, the Hispanics, the Muslims, ect., out of one's country. But you have to ask yourself the question what happens after that goal is achieved? Does ethnic cleansing create a homogenous racial society as some of the Far Right organizations speculate? It seems to me that the white nationalists never seem to have an answer - they think strictly in terms of the short term goals, but forget to see the long term effects of such a move.

Even a thorough-going ethnic cleansing of non-whites will not overcome social alienation. Much of the social pathologies in the West can be traced back to the individual's isolation and alienation from his community. But 'nationalist communitarianism' will give him true democracy, true freedom, i.e., a sense of belonging to his own culture. Once he feels responsibility to his own culture, he will be less inclined to engage in destructive activities against it.

It is true that white nationalism, and Far Right populism, claim to stand for roughly the same things as de Benoist. That is, they want to overcome the individual's social isolation by encouraging him to feel a sense of belonging to one's race or nation. But there have been many white societies where individuals still felt that social alienation - one has to look at the all white societies of the West in the 1950s and 1960s. On top of that, the conventional Far Right ideologies seem to attract individuals who are not the most upstanding examples of their race or nation - white nationalism, bluntly, often ends up attracting white trash.

Many of the Far Right populist politicians in Europe, the USA and Australia seem to want a return to the bourgeois, halcyon days of the 1950s, which were whiter, cleaner and safer, but hardly communitarian.

After all, if Britain or West Germany in the 1950s and 1960s did possess a real sense of communal identity and purpose, they wouldn't have let in all the immigrants in the first place.

So it could be that de Benoist's ideas are superior to the conventional Far Right ideologies existing in the present. It cannot be said that De Benoist-ism has been tried and found wanting. Perhaps 'ethnic federalism' will attract more people to the Far Right in the West - the right sort of people, too.

The unique thing about de Benoist's philosophy is that it is neither white nationalist nor multiculturalist – it stands in between. As such, it represents a third position. Certainly, the enemies of the Far Right will not be ready to deal with such a stance; the old white nationalism is very familiar to them, but de Benoist is something new.

That is another reason why he is to be recommended.

3

THE RADICALISATION OF THE MIDDLE CLASSES

"...National Socialism is not merely a political and economic upheaval but a social revolution as well. To a very large extent it has brought the lower middle class into power. To be sure, one finds quite a few aristocrats and intellectuals in the Nazi regime. Furthermore, there are plenty of Nazis sprung from peasant or worker stock, some of whom, like the Weimar Gauleiter, would rise in any society. Yet the lower middle class seems to be inordinately in evidence. One does not notice this so much in Berlin, because the ablest elements in the Party tend to gravitate to the seat of power. In the provinces the Spiessbürgertum comes much more to the front." - Lothrop Stoddard, "Into the Darkness" (1940)

Recently, the Sydney Forum hosted Professor Andrew Fraser, who gave an illuminating speech on, among other things, non-white immigration into Australia. He took the position that the 'Anglo-European' Australians (as he calls them) ought to resist the immigrant tide. But, he asked, how are the masses, or a significant proportion of them, to be mobilized into taking action? He declared that he did not, at present, have the answer. He did suggest, however, that, as a first step, nationalists should be aiming at a movement, at building a groundswell of support, before forming a political party; nationalism, he said, should be extra-parliamentary.

Another point that emerged, during discussions with other members attending the Forum (after the presentations by the guest speakers were over) was that a clear difference exists between radical and reactionary nationalists. A perfect example of the latter is Pauline Hanson, who, it could be argued, was a reactionary as well as an agrarian socialist. (One can be a socialist – i.e., demand a redistribution of wealth - and be, at the same time, reactionary).Reactionary nationalists want to turn the clock back to an idealized Australia (or France or Germany) of the recent past. In the Australian case, they celebrate the parochial folk culture of Australia – i.e., use Ned Kelly and other Australian folk figures in their iconography.

The radical nationalists, on the other hand, want a progressive movement forward - more than that, a complete break from the past and its traditions. We can classify Mussolini, Robert Mugabe, Che Guevara, Mao Tse Tung, and Hugo Chavez as men who are nationalists, radicals and socialists.

(Perhaps a clearer illustration of the difference that exists between a radical and a non-radical lies in the split in the mainstream Left in the West in the late sixties and early sixties. One side of the Left - the reformist - advocated working within the system and making changes within the context of liberal parliamentary democracy. Their tendency, even if they were communist, was to join the Democrats in the USA or the Labor Party in Australia and attempt to steer the ideology of those organizations towards communism.

On the other hand, the more radical Left advocated extra-parliamentary 'direct action' - the most spectacular examples of which were urban guerrilla terrorism. Examples of urban guerilla radical groups are Baader-Meinhof in Germany, the Weathermen in the United States, the Red Brigades in Italy, and the Tupamaros in Uruguay).

One can see, from this example that a world of difference exists between the radicals of the Left and the reformists and moderates. Even if the moderates, in this case, sympathize with Trotsky and Mao - both radicals - they are still moderate by dint of their actions.

It occurred to me, after the Forum and the subsequent discussions, that the history and ideas of the Left, particularly the New Left, have a great deal of relevance to nationalism today in Australia and the rest of the Western world. Throughout this article I will be using standard terms most often found in Marxism - 'Left', 'Right', 'working-class', 'middle-class', 'bourgeois', etc. - but without any evaluative tone. That is, I will not be using the word 'middle-class' as a term of opprobrium, as the communists and some neo-fascist intellectuals, such as Evola, do.

These words shall be used as descriptive tools only.

A relevant text for the purposes of this article is Georges Sorel's Reflections on Violence (1908), which tackles some of the problems raised by Marxism - in particular, the failure of the working-classes to behave as the Marxist theory predicted. One of his conclusions was that attempts to bring about class consciousness through pure theory were doomed to fail. What mattered was an enabling 'myth', an idea which would induce class-consciousness among the proletariat, force them to undertake direct action against capitalism, and bring about revolution.

Sorel's solution - a syndicalist one - was the general strike, which would bring about all the conditions needed for the formation of class-consciousness, class-war, etc.

The advantage of Sorel's approach was its simplicity and directness. Modern Leftist groups try and bring about revolution by handing out issues of the Green Left Weekly on university campuses - when little to no proletarians are in attendance at those universities, and, in any case, have little interest in a refried Leninism. The Socialist Alliance also gets involved in campaigns to end sanctions against Iran, or get the Australian government to take Hezbollah off its list of terrorist groups - which is all very worthy, but has little to do with socialism, and again, fails to get the attention of the Australian working-classes. What the Australian communists need is a catalyst, a trigger which, like Sorel's general strike, brings about the conditions of change in one stroke.

Like the communists, the Australian nationalists are looking for a catalyst. They have in mind a revolution - a racial revolution - in which white Australians will suddenly develop racial consciousness and sweep all the non-white immigrants away. Cronulla, for a time, seemed to be such a trigger event. Other racialists take a more gradualist approach: the white masses will develop race-consciousness, and then embark on a racial revolution, but only after non-white immigration gets to the point that it becomes unbearable. This is similar to the Marxist theory - that capitalist societies will inevitably become communist ones because of the progressive 'immiseration' of the working-classes, which continually lowers their living standards.

There are a number of problems with the Australian (and in general, white nationalist) approach. Without a doubt, endless non-white immigration has seen to a progressive deterioration in the quality of life in Western societies, and even mainstream politicians and media commentators (in, for instance, Britain, where the effects of immigration in the past ten years have been profound) are beginning to remark on that fact, or at least discuss it. But, by itself, immigration is not sufficient to bring about the revolution the white nationalists (or at least the more radical of them) are seeking. If one has a distaste for living and working among non-white people, one can simply move to a more white area - or a more white country. It may well be that the immigration of Sudanese asylum-seekers will expand to the point where whites have nowhere left to live; the pinch on available land and resources will be such that whites are forced to take action. But that, at present, is in the far future.

I myself believe, too, that the predictions of the demographers, who say that the British will be a minority in their own country by 2050, are too apocalyptic. Yes, immigration will continue to rise; but whites are not at the point of being bred out. (Even Bill White has written a number of articles arguing for this point). Which is not to say that immigration is not a pressing issue: it is. But it is not pressing enough for the white masses to rise up and do anything about it.

In order to get any group to take action - and here my analysis shows a trace of Marxism - their economic interests have to be affected. Economics also has a history of remarkable success in mobilizing the disparate members of an ethnic group towards the same objective. Marx believed that capitalism, by affecting the working-classes economically, would be sufficient to make the proletariat realize that they share a common interest. Likewise, the economic effects of capitalism can unify members of an ethnic group. A case in point is the coup against the ethnic-Indian dominated Chaudry government in Fiji in 2000. George Speight and a number of other black Fijians stormed the parliament and held members of the government hostage for nearly two months, and Chaudry's government was overthrown in a military coup. What was the motive behind the coup? Simply that the economic interests of black Fijians were being affected. The Fijian constitution enforces black Fijian ownership of 83 per cent of land; Chaudry's government, it was felt, would introduce land reform - with the inevitable result that the hard-working and clannish ethnic Indians would buy up all the land.

The Speight coup is something white nationalists can only dream about. Speight managed to mobilize a large segment of his ethnic group behind him and overthrow the existing government (dominated by members of a foreign ethnic group) with ease. The key to his success was that his ethnic group saw that their economic interests would be endangered by a free-market economic system, in which Indians could buy all the land they wanted from Fijians; and so they gave him support.

I am not suggesting that nationalists here in Australia, or Europe or America, follow Speight's methods. I am using the Speight case to suggest that a serious racialist political attitude comes from socialism, or rather, a determination to protect the economic interests of one's racial or ethnic group against competition from outsiders. At the Sydney Forum, nationalist activists decried the fact that it is hard, these days, to mobilize 'decent people' to take up arms for the movement; that it was difficult to get women involved. Instead of reaching a wide cross-section of society, modern nationalism in the West seems to reach only a small proportion. (In an article by the New Right Australia New Zealand, titled 'Freaks in the Movement", it has been argued that that small proportion is primarily made up of the underclass - the working poor and the welfare class). The reason why is that nationalism is not appealing to the economic self-interest.

Nothing, in my experience, motivates middle-class Australian women more than the threat of immigration from the Sub-Continent - of Pakistanis and Indians and competing with them for the same jobs and the same contracts in I.T., law, medicine, finance, small business, engineering, and science. We need plenty of members of that demographic - white-middle class women (and men) in the movement, but we are not getting them because we are not addressing their economic concerns.

The white Australian middle-classes dislike Sudanese asylum-seekers, and Vietnamese and Lebanese on welfare, but cannot be expected to be passionate about these issues. Why? Because the middle-classes are not welfare recipients, and are not competing against those migrants for state aid! But they are competing, in the field of business, against immigrants from the Sub-Continent.

(Perhaps one of the defects of nationalism in Europe is that it concentrates too much on immigrants who hail from the Middle East and North Africa. Arab, Kurdish, Turkish and African immigrants want to immigrate to Europe in order to get jobs in the low-wage service sector or to go on welfare. The economic interests of the middle-classes are thereby unaffected, even though these immigrants may become a social problem – i.e., they go out and commit crimes. To my knowledge, the North African and Middle Eastern immigrants in France are confined to huge urban ghettoes and only infrequently come into contact with the white French. So they do not present a direct economic threat, either to the French working- or middle-classes).

This article does not aim at giving solutions to all the problems which afflict the nationalist movement; it, rather, aims at giving a clear statement of the problem. We have to clearly outline, among ourselves, what it is that we want. Once we have determined our goal, we can canvas the various means of reaching it.

The Marxists have a number of means of reaching their goal: some favor infiltrating liberal democratic parties; others, trade unionism; others, 'direct action'; others, terrorism; and so on. But, unlike the Marxists, we nationalists are not exactly sure of our goal.

What is it then? What is it that we want? I think we can summarize it as follows. We want a nationalism which is in keeping with historic Western and European nationalism of the past and present - European fascism, post-war neo-fascism and the Nouvelle Droite and thinkers in that circle (such as Guillaume Faye); a nationalism which is in tune with modern economic, social and geopolitical realities; a nationalism which is radical, not reactionary; a nationalism which has its base in the middle-classes; a nationalism which is socialist and left-wing.

The last of these needs some explanation. Socialism means a number of things: it means the redistribution of wealth through taxes, transfers and nationalizations, to a favored sectional interest (in the case of Marxism, the working-class; in the case of the nationalism I am proposing, the middle-class). It also means protecting that favored interest from competition (in the case of Marxism, cheap, imported and usually low-skilled labor) and maintaining the economic position of that interest against changes brought on by the market or by recession. The main threat to the position of the white-collar middle-class today is from non-white migrants, usually from the Sub-Continent (but not restricted to there).

Competition from that source will undercut the wages and living conditions of the white-collar class, and damage the country's national and cultural cohesiveness as a whole. So our socialism would oppose that form of migration, perhaps more vehemently than migration from Sudan or Kurdistan.

Which is not to say that migration from Africa or the Middle East is not a problem - of course it is - but the failure to address middle-class concerns is one of the reasons why nationalism has made so little headway in Australia and, perhaps, in Europe and North America as well. It is only by addressing the bread and butter issues, and the concerns of the class we most need to have on our side - the middle-class - that nationalism will become a mass movement, and then, after a sufficient period of growth, an electoral movement.

Once we have worked out the basics of what we want from nationalism, we can then go on to debate the means by which we will attain our goals. Hugo Chavez, for example, knows exactly what he wants: he wants to redistribute his country's wealth to his electoral base, the Venezuelan poor, in particular, the slum-dwellers of the urban centers like Caracas. He uses a variety of methods to achieve that goal, never confining himself to one, but can only do so with some success because he knows what he wants.

I am not here, in this article, proposing any means; only ends. Once the nationalists here in Australia and in the Western world know what they want and can state their aims and goals with some clarity, we can proceed.

Otherwise we will be, like in the past decades, barking up the wrong tree and go nowhere.

4

ON KAMERADSCHAFT

This is an article about German nationalism - specifically, about the Nationaldemokratische Partei Deutschlands (NPD) - and what other nationalists outside Germany can learn from the NPD's practical approach to politics and creating a 'parallel society'.

The NPD has been achieving good results in German state elections recently, and may even do well in upcoming federal elections. But, aside from some electoral success (which is not as hard as one might think for the 'Far Right' to achieve in Europe), the NPD have experienced some success in building up a mass support base in Germany as well - an extra-parliamentary support base. Their thinking is that nationalism must first become a popular mass movement as well as an electoral one: it is this that should be given a priority.

Nationalists, of course, are aware of how adverse the political situation is for nationalism in Germany. It is a general rule, I think, of modern politics that the more strategically important a country is in the nationalist struggle, the more repressive it will be.

France and Germany, by my own estimation, are the most repressive states on the Continent. Which is not to say that censorship and persecution are not equally strong elsewhere: but that the liberal-Zionist establishment seems to stand to lose more if France and Germany go nationalist, the two countries being widely acknowledged as the two leading powers on the Continent? It is fair to say that were nationalists to gain power in France and Germany, followed by Britain, Spain and Italy, the other European countries would fall like dominoes – Europe itself would see a pan-European nationalist revolution. This is why the liberal, pro-USA and pro-Israel establishment devotes so much time to persecuting and censoring nationalists in France and Germany.

But this alone does not explain, I think, precisely why the nationalist struggle in Germany in particular is so important. Most nationalists are very sympathetic to German nationalism, out of a sense of solidarity: which is why Le Pen's Front National, and the British National Party, for example, cultivate ties with the NPD. But, surprisingly enough, there is little evidence of any desire to imitate the 'German model' of post war nationalism, which is surprising, considering the number of Nutzis, for instance, who are present in the movement.

But it is evident that the Nutzis are only interested in one period of German history – the period of the Third Reich, and its inception - and in nothing that came before or after; their desire is to bring about another Hitlerian revolution (what Francis Parker Yockey called 'The European Revolution of 1933') in 'white' countries across the world. Everything is interpreted through the Nutzi ideological prism: Bill White's website, www.overthrow.com, regularly classifies the NPD as a 'National Socialist' party – i.e., Nutzi and American. One would expect the Nutzis to display some form of Germanophilism, an exaggerated respect for German political and cultural achievements (which one finds in the thinking of Houston Stewart Chamberlain and Yockey, both non-Germans). But, ironically, Nutzism and its related 'white power'/white nationalist offshoots have very little interest in German nationalism since the war.

The position I will be taking in this article is a very unusual one and might be hard to understand for non Germans. I am recommending here that nationalist movements outside of Germany pay attention to the 'German model' and deliberately isolate some of its elements and incorporate them into their own ideologies and practices; their aim should be to minimize the parochial elements unique to their own countries (America, France, Australia or whatever) and become more 'German' and more 'Prussian'.

Our starting point here is Spengler's famous essay 'Prussianism and Socialism' (1920). Spengler's essay can be seen as a sketch of a certain economic and social system which was later embodied in German

National Socialism. But it was more than an economic program, but a style of life, which transcends National Socialism. The Nutzis who appropriate National Socialist uniforms and symbols are using the outer trappings of 'Prussianism', leaving the basics and fundamentals untouched. The German Nationalists, today's NPD, and the German trade unions led by August Bebel (a figure praised by Spengler) contain the German or 'Prussian' spirit, which Spengler describes as follows:

I should like to make clear what I mean by the term "Prussianism." The name, of course, refers to an area of Europe where certain attitudes took on impressive shape and began to evolve. But Prussianism is, first and foremost, a feeling, an instinct, a compulsion. It is the embodiment of spiritual and intellectual traits—and that means also of certain physical qualities—that have long since become the distinguishing characteristics of a race, or rather of the best and most typical representatives of this race. Certainly not every person born in England is "English" in the racial sense; and not everyone born in Prussia in genuinely "Prussian." This word denotes everything we Germans possess by way of destiny, will, inner drive, and ability, and nothing of our vague ideas, desires, and whims. There are true Prussian types in all of Germany—I am thinking of men like Friedrich List and Hegel, of certain inventors, scholars, engineers, and organizers, but especially of a particular type of German worker. Since the Battles of Rossbach and Leuthen there have been many Germans who in the depth of their souls have harbored a small strain of Prussianism, a potential source of energy which can become active at great moments of history.

As yet, however, the only real Prussian achievements have been the creations of Frederick William I and Frederick the Great: the Prussian state and the Prussian people. ('Prussians and Englishmen', 11, in 'Prussianism and Socialism')

He goes on to say that:

To the Prussian way of thinking, the will of the individual is subsumed under the will of the totality.

The officers' corps, the members of the civil service branches, August Bebel's army of workers, and ultimately the German Volk of 1813, 1870, and 1914 have all felt, willed, and acted as a suprapersonal unity. This is not just herd instinct; it is an expression of sublime strength and freedom, something which the outsider can never understand. Prussianism is exclusive. Even in its proletarian form it rejects the workers of other countries together with their egoistic pseudo-socialism. ('Prussians and Englishmen', 13)

The essential thing is that such a spirit exists beyond a program, or even a party which competes against other parties in elections. As Spengler writes:

Socialism, i.e., Prussianism as it is not yet understood, is a real entity of the highest order.

Marxism is literature. Literature can become obsolete; reality either conquers or dies. We need only compare socialist criticism as it is heard at international conventions with but one socialist fact, the party of August Bebel. The popular phrase about ideas making history, when understood as it should be, is nothing but the special pleading of literary gossips. Ideas cannot be expressed. An artist can see them, a thinker can feel them, a statesman or soldier can make them real. Ideas become conscious only through the blood—instinctively, not by means of abstract contemplation. They make their existence known by the life style of peoples, the symbolism of deeds and accomplishments. And whether or not people are aware of them, either correctly or falsely, is a trifling matter. ('Marx', 21, in 'Prussianism and Socialism')

So, this is what the NPD possesses which many other nationalist organizations outside of Germany do not: a uniquely Prussian and communitarian (if we reject the Blairite overtones of such a word) spirit. This manifests itself in the NPD's extra-parliamentary activities, especially in the eastern parts of Germany: it runs kindergartens, discos, youth groups, community volunteer organizations which assist pensioners... Volunteer organizations like the fire brigades, Technische Hilfswerk (a equivalent of the Australian SES), Red Cross, etc, are full of nationalists and in some parts of Germany these organizations are fully controlled by nationalists.

The 'infiltration' of nationalists became such a problem that in 2005 the interior minister of Brandenburg, a state in the eastern part of Germany, called for the banning of nationalists in any volunteer organization. Unfortunately for the minister this was rebuked by the very same volunteer organizations with the warning that if nationalists should be not allowed to become members the services would have such a shortage of volunteers that many units would not be able to function.

These techniques for building up grass-roots support are nothing new: after all, the Italian Fascists and the German National Socialists used them, and had borrowed them from the Italian and German communist parties. But the essential thing is that the NPD uses them in the service of an Idea (as Spengler defines them): which, if put into words, is to be expressed (vaguely) as feeling of Volksgemeinschaft, or Kameradschaft, of Germans helping other Germans. Moreover, this is done in a disciplined (I should say self-disciplined) and almost militaristic manner, and out of a sense of duty. Spengler writes that:

Service—that is the style of Old Prussia, similar to that of Old Spain, which also created a people by engaging in knightly warfare against the heathen. Not "I" but "we"—a feeling of community to which every individual sacrifices his whole being. The individual does not matter; he must offer himself to the totality. All exist for all, and all partake of that glorious inner freedom, the libertas oboe dientiae which has always distinguished the best exemplars of Prussian breeding. The Prussian army, Prussian civil service, and August Bebel's workers' brigades are all products of this breeding principle. ('Prussians and Englishmen', 12)

This is pre-State politics, pre-parliamentary politics. It shows that, in order to be 'nationalist' in Germany, one need not have control of parliament; that or a massive army of panzers and Messerschmitts.

The 'Prussianism' of the German people can be expressed in an extra-parliamentarian and communitarian way, by small actions which, taken together, benefit the totality. The NPD understood that grass roots level involvement is the key to electoral success. While all the other parties talk about the problems in the society, the NPD and other nationalists work in and within the community to solve the problems first hand.

Media commentators are always remarking that the German economy is a mess, which is true. Germany, like France, is one of the richest countries in the world, but has high unemployment and low levels of economic growth. It would be easy to blame this on purely economic causes, as the critics of the German government want to do; certainly, Chancellor Angela Merkel's tax hikes have made the German economy (already unhealthy under Schröder) worse. The economists prescribe solutions which are purely economical: cut taxes, get rid of the excessive restrictions on hiring and firing workers, and cut down on the excessive social security contributions employers are forced to pay, and the German economy will be fine again. Because of the increased economic growth, Germans will be too busy enjoying themselves to notice the creeping immigration problem (and the economic growth will only attract more immigrants).

And, not only will the immigration problem recede from the consciousness of the average German, so will Germany's servitude to Israel and America, forced upon it by Germany's defeat in the war and sixty years of Holocaust-brainwashing. What German would care about redressing past historical injustices – e.g., the expulsion of the Germans from the East, or the Morgenthau Plan - when he is making money?

This is more or less the plan the liberal-democrats have for Germany (and for France and the other 'sick' countries of Europe). Economic growth, and a solution to Germany's unemployment problem, is desirable, of course. But it is likely that neither will be achieved under Merkel's government, or the one after that, or the one after that. The Germans, at this point in time, have an inability to get their act together. What is lacking is not only decisiveness, but, importantly, a feeling of goodwill, or, as I would put it, Volksgemeinschaft.

The enemies of German nationalism are always comparing today's economic circumstances to that of 1932: each election victory by the so-called "Far Right" is a sign of "rising Neo-Nazism" which will see the arrival of a "Fourth Reich", and so on. This is all nonsense, of course: but one similarity exists between the Germany of 2006 and the Germany of 1932, and that is the absence of the feeling of a Volksgemeinschaft. The German National Socialists were accused of having a rather vague program before they took office; that is, they did not have a plan. But they did have a sense of Volksgemeinschaft, and it was their appeal to Germany - their call for Germans to start helping other Germans - which led to the turnaround in the German economy. It was the same spirit which existed in the catastrophic aftermath of WWII and the deliberate devastation of Germany through the Morgenthau Plan - that this time the Germans will pull through, through co-operation and effort.

One cannot induce that spirit through self-abnegation - self-abnegation which exists in Germany today, where Turkish immigrants are considered "German" and massive government funds are earmarked as compensation payments to Jews who were "gassed" by Germans during the war (and then many turned up alive again). Germany's economic problems go beyond the economy - it is not merely a matter of taxes and trade union laws.

But the same applies to the rest of Europe. Britain, for instance, has low unemployment figures (at least on paper); but it suffers from more or less the same problems as does Germany - for one, social isolation and a paralysis in the face of immigration, which erodes the British identity and threatens to depopulate the British Isles of white Britons altogether. Just as serious is the sordidness of British life, especially British urban life. This is symbolized by the rise of the 'chav' - the Briton who dresses up as a Negro, engages in petty and violent crime, destroys himself through drink and drugs, fathers illegitimate children (all supported by the welfare state) and drops out of school in his teens.

We are seeing the rise here of a new social type, a new type of 'Untermenschen', which will spread to the Continent as well. These problems are exacerbated, in Britain, by a traditional spirit of liberal individualism, which, as Spengler would say, is part of the British soul, as it were. But again, they can be partly relieved by the infusion of Volksgemeinschaft - imported from Germany. The same goes for France, and the same for Spain and Italy.

The key is for nationalists to organize themselves into hierarchical, disciplined, extra-parliamentary communitarian organizations - activist organizations. This spreads the word on the ground that nationalism (whether it be in Australia, Britain, France or Spain) is a good thing - that the media is distorting nationalism when it portrays it as the exclusive domain of skinheads intent on beating up foreigners. But, more than a good public relations exercise, such activism also embodies a new Idea - the Prussian Idea - of self-sacrifice and dedication to the good of one's community. (It goes without saying that this is the community which is indigenous to those countries - not the community of Kurdish asylum seekers or Albanian day laborers).

At this point, the reader will be wondering how a French nationalist can become 'Prussian', if 'Prussianism', as Spengler defines it, is something so uniquely German. But, while 'Prussianism' is of the blood, it can be transferred. Yockey wrote that Mussolini 'Effected the transformation of Italy by infusing it with the Prussian-German Socialist Ethos' ('Stronger Power-Currents in an Age of Absolute Politics' in 'The Enemy of Europe'), in the 1920s, and that 'In this century, it is of scant importance what language a European speaks and in what geographic area he was brought up. Of importance only is the spirituality that permeates his inner life. Europe's Churchills and Toynes prove that it is possible for Americans to be born and raised in Europe. The example of Mussolini shows that an ethical Prussian can be born and raised in the Romagna, and the examples of Ezra Pound, William Joyce, Robert Best, Douglas Chandler, and others show that Europeans can be born or raised in America'. ('The Demise of the Western Nations' in 'The Enemy of Europe')

Indeed, I would argue that all of the fascism of Europe in the 1930s and 1940s was an expression of the German Idea - that Mosley, Mussolini, Quisling and the rest were 'Prussian' in the same way that Mussolini was. But one of the main differences between European nationalism then and now is that the fascists were proponents of corporatist economic programs, of remodeling Europe's capitalist economies on the basis of the corporatist guilds of the Middle Ages. Even the post-war theorists of neo-fascism, such as Yockey and Evola, were attracted to the idea. But this essay is not endorsing corporatism, or any economic program - or, indeed, any program which can be expressed in a political manifesto for an organization trying to get itself elected to parliament. One of the shortcomings of modern nationalism is that it thinks too much of these things: draw up a manifesto, and try to get elected with it - as if this were the way that politics works.

The NPD's approach, on the other hand, is to concentrate on three battles: the battles for the streets of Germany, the battles for the minds of the intellectuals and, finally, the battle for the parliaments.

Again, community-based activism is something that the Maoists, for instance, attempt to do; but their main tool is guerrilla warfare and intimidation of the peasant population. After the rural areas have been won over, the Maoist insurgency can concentrate on the cities, in particular, the capital. We nationalists, of course, differ from the Maoists in our choice of means and ends; but the idea of 'communities first' is a good one. Nationalism has to be expressed as a style, as a way of life, before it can become an electoral movement.

Before drafting this essay, I discussed the idea of Volksgemeinschaft, and what the German nationalists were attempting to do with it, with an apolitical friend. He accused us, German nationalists, of using a myth - of a uniquely German or 'Prussian' spirit – which did not in fact exist. The German nationalists were creating Volksgemeinschaft through the act of living it. I could have argued with him that 'Prussianism' is not a fiction; but this would have been beside the point. The Holocaust, one could argue, is an extrapolation, but it has been an extremely profitable one for the Jews and one which has brought post-war Germany (and Europe) to its knees; Zionism, or rather, the Jewish claim to Palestine, is a myth, but it is one that ethnically cleansed hundreds of thousands of Palestinians from the former Palestine and led to the creation of the most powerful State in the Western world.

So how can nationalists here in Australia imitate the German example? The essential thing is to take small steps at the beginning. Nationalists can buy goods and services off other nationalists. (For instance, at a skinhead concert, a tattooist was pointed out to me as a fellow nationalist. If I wanted a tattoo, I was told, I should go this man. And indeed I should: why spend money on a tattooist who is apolitical or not a nationalist?). Nationalists can also join volunteer community organizations - such as volunteer fire brigades, the SES, Red Cross, Scout groups, etc.

Unions, too, are examples of large, extra-parliamentary, community-based organizations (which is why communists have traditionally spent so much time and effort infiltrating them). Suppose that one powerful trade union had a hundred, or two hundred, or more, nationalist activists - that would be a powerful force. (It need not even be a blue-collar union - imagine if the white-collar financial services unions had a large nationalist membership). There are many possibilities in this direction.

Equally as important, if not more so, is to break down stereotypes of what a nationalist is. On Jewish-produced TV shows and in Hollywood movies ('American History X', 'Oz', and so forth), nationalists are portrayed as skinhead misfits who end up in jail, for instance. With her lowbrow and populist attitude, Pauline Hanson reinforced the notion of Australian nationalists as being stupid (and a few are - but there are many stupid leftists, as well). When meeting non-nationalists, it is important to make a positive first impression as a person, as a human being - and then let them know that you are nationalist. Often they are surprised that someone with education, and a good job, can be a nationalist. Their perception, fed by the Jewish-owned media, is that anyone who is an 'extreme' nationalist is a "Nazi" who is covered in swastika tattoos, etc. So the discovery that a normal, decent intelligent human being can be a so-called "Nazi" is a big shock to them.

Politics is not a collection of truths, but of facts, as Spengler would say. What matters is what is done.

The German nationalists have very little: not much in the way of an intellectual, worked-out ideology (in the way that the Marxists do); they cannot use uniforms, or salutes, and, for their national flags, must use old German Imperial flags as a symbol of Germany before it was reduced to vassaldom. But, in their discipline and their service to the community, in their comradeship, they represent the true Germany, the German Idea.

And this is what matters; the organization of the German people into a community which does not hate itself, which thinks and acts as a totality. Never mind the fact that today's Germans do not see themselves as 'Prussian' and hate themselves and their history; so long as a small minority is the standard-bearer of the German Idea, Germany is preserved. By liberating Germany from bondage to NATO and Israel, and reconstructing a new Germany (really the old Germany) on the basis of Volksgemeinschaft, the German nationalists will liberate Europe and the West as well - but only if nationalists worldwide follow their example.

5

ON NATIONALISM AND THE SOCIAL QUESTION

The great Austrian political thinker and champion of free-market liberalism, F.A. von Hayek, made a famous distinction in his work between 'values' and 'merits', summed up in his famous slogan 'There is no value to society'. (Margaret Thatcher was attempting to convey the same idea when she made her famous assertion that 'There is no such thing as society'). Hayek argued that, when we assess the worth of a man's labors - in providing us with symphonies, or paintings, or glass etchings, or plumbing, or shoes, or whatever - the marketplace provides us with the only accurate assessment of their value. The market, which is made up of individual buyers and sellers, assesses the value of, say, a pair of shoes at $90. If buyers disagree with the price charged by the shoe seller, the latter must drop his price, and sell at a discount, if he wants to move his product off the shelves. If he refuses to budge on prices, or if he is underestimated the demand for his product (mistakenly believing that there is a large demand for his shoes, when there wasn't) he goes out of business.

But, says Hayek, suppose we take the socialist point of view and say that the shoe seller is a meritorious individual - that he deserves a 'better' price for his shoes than the one consumers are accustomed to paying, or that he deserves to have shoes sold in amounts large enough to make him wealthy. We are then assessing the shoe seller's labor on the basis of 'merit' and not 'value'. Hayek's point is that such an assessment is entirely subjective: the shoe seller and his friends and family may believe that he is meritorious, and deserves to make more money than he does; but the buyers in the market may have an entirely different valuation. The consequence of this is that it is impossible to get all parties to come to an agreement on 'merit'; but it is entirely possible to get all parties to come an agreement on 'value' - and such an agreement happens every day, in the market. Hayek believes that we cannot assess the 'value' of 'society' (or a something 'socially useful', 'socially beneficial') in that same impersonal (and clear-cut) way. Hence, 'there is no value to society'.

Hayek makes a similar distinction between an economy based on 'needs' and 'wants'. Joe Bloggs, an abattoir worker who lives in Cowra, needs a job in Cowra - otherwise he will be forced to move elsewhere to look for work, or take up a different career. In an economy based on 'needs', the government will ensure that Joe Bloggs is given that job. But suppose that there is not enough consumer demand for meat from Cowra: the abattoir will be forced to close down because of the impersonal pressure of the market. In an economy based on consumer 'wants', the government will allow the abattoir to close down and will do nothing for Joe Bloggs or the other abattoir workers.

Similarly, people in sparsely-populated rural areas may demand phone coverage from the national telephone companies, which are reluctant to service those areas because there will be no profit in doing so. In an economy based on 'wants', the rural population will have to go without phone coverage, or move to the city where they can obtain it; in an economy based on 'needs', the government will ensure that they are provided with phone coverage.

What relevance does this all have to nationalism? A great deal! Even the self proclaimed Neo-Nazi Bill White writes that:

Even race, while fundamental to the National Socialist worldview is not central to the National Socialist argument. When I talk to my organizers -- and check out our mailing list on Yahoo groups if you want confirmation -- I don't tell them to talk about race first, or immigration first, or any of these other issues first when trying to communicate the advantages of National Socialism to white people. I tell them to talk about the economy first -- in all its aspects -- and from there to point at the Jews, and then to show how Jewish connection to racial issues, and social-cultural issues, and political issues "trickles down" and reveals their poison in every aspect.

As has been written here at the New Right Australia/New Zealand site many times, National Socialism and Italian Fascism enjoyed their success first and foremost because they were social and economic doctrines first, and everything else second. The question - 'Do we want an economy based on needs, or wants?' - is as relevant today for nationalists as it was in 1933 or 1922.

The mainstream Right believes that we should have an economy based on consumer wants; the mainstream Left, one based on 'human' and 'social' needs. It is held, by a good many media commentators and intellectuals, that the Right has won the debate on the global economy; the twentieth century was the century of socialism, but, in the end, communism imploded from within, unable to compete with the Western capitalist economies. Even the West had to adopt, after the crises of the 1970s, competition and deregulation - inevitable 'market reforms' - in order to survive and prosper. America and the UK do well, it is argued, because they adopted the 'reform' path; Germany, France and other Continental countries have stagnated because of their adherence to the old welfare-state socialism.

The purpose of this article is not to revisit that old and hackneyed debate: it has received enough attention from mainstream journalists and intellectuals in the past twenty-five years. The intention of this article is to look at the place of the 'needs versus wants' and the 'merit versus value' debate within the context of the nationalist political struggle.

Now, in 2007, we can look at the benefits, and drawbacks, of economic systems such as communism and fascism with more perspective than, for instance, the people living in the 1930s and 1940s. The general consensus, in the mainstream Western media, is that communism has failed - and it is a view I, like many other nationalists, share. Take, for example, Mao's China. The difference between Maoist Marxism and ordinary Marxism was that the former championed the peasant, the latter the blue-collar laborer: Maoism could be described accurately as Marxism for the peasant class - it sought, not a 'dictatorship of the proletariat', but a 'dictatorship of the peasants' (or, more accurately, a dictatorship of an elite group of intellectuals who would rule in the name of the peasants). That was the official Maoist party line (we know, however, that Mao cared little for the peasants, and was interested foremost in making China a great geopolitical force, capable of being a rival to both Russia and America). At any rate, Mao's economic policies were disastrous for Chinese peasantry: under the Great Leap Forward, for instance, millions of them starved to death, mainly thanks to economic bungling and neglect (which occurs too often under communism). No greater example of communist failure can be found: after all, communism, ostensibly, intends to improve the national standard of living, and one of the main arguments against capitalism is that it leads to poverty and misery. But communism - as we have seen from the example of China, North Korea, the Soviet Union, Cambodia and the African states which turned communist - led to even more poverty and misery than capitalism, and starvation on a hitherto unimagined scale.

Now, in the 2000s, China has been forced to adopt the market mechanism as an alternative to socialism; eventually it will move further and further from an economy geared towards satisfying 'needs' and to one which aims at satisfying 'wants'. Vietnam has done the same; only Cuba and North Korea remain as the last hold-outs.

Communism could have been expected to do well in Europe: after all, even the economically backward countries of Eastern Europe are far more developed than, for instance, China at the time of the communist revolution. Again, naive left-wingers in the West supported the Soviet Union in its war against Germany because they believed that the communist system was better: the fascists were tools of capitalism (so the party line went), and capitalism always leads to poverty, misery, injustice, inequality, etc. But, once the war was over, and the Red Army had conquered Germany and Eastern Europe, it turned out that communism as an economic system wasn't as good as capitalism or fascism; it was downright inferior. On a simple, day to day level, the standard of living was below that of the Western European countries: East Germany produced unreliable and inefficient state-designed cars, and built shoddy housing; and shoddy and inefficient consumer goods were the general rule throughout the whole Eastern bloc. No communist in the West would have been able to cope for long living in an Eastern bloc country, simply because of the vastly inferior standard of living. Communism in Eastern Europe, and the Soviet Union, declined for a number of reasons: but one of the main reasons is that, simply, the populations there wanted the lifestyle of the West: better cars, better clothes, better houses, reliable supplies of electricity, gas, and water...

For this reason, the communist parties in the West are, after the post-1989 collapse of Soviet communism, unpopular. That is, they do not have a mass base of support. Communist organizations may be active in student politics on university campuses; their refried Trotskyism manages to attract its share of followers (from my experience) of naive and politically uneducated youth. But it is out of the question that they will ever be able to win power in Australia or in any other Western country. The reason for that is that we all know, by now, that communism doesn't work. Or, rather, the price demanded by communism is too high for Westerners to pay; for one thing, our glitzy shopping malls will have to go (to be replaced, presumably, by state-owned malls selling state-made jeans), and not even the most hardcore Leftist university student wants that. Communist activism in the West is one exercise in futility.

The reality is that, in Australia and most other Western countries, is that the Hayekian neoliberals have won for the most part. For the past 11 years, a conservative center-right government has actively striven to introduce competition. It has broken, for the most part, the trade unions' grip on the labor market, has allowed competition in various industries (including the dairy industry) and is now in the process of dismantling a price-support scheme for Australian farmers (which makes it illegal for farmers to sell their wheat overseas below a fixed price) which has existed for 67 years. It has also kept up the policy, introduced by successive Australian post-war governments, of free trade, and privatized the national telephone company.

The social democratic Labor Party, and members of the agrarian-socialist National Party (which, ironically, is in coalition with the conservatives), oppose these policies; many nationalists here in Australia oppose these policies as well. But my own reaction is: so what. The Labor Party, of course, opposes deregulation of the labor market because it is run by trade unionists who want to preserve their monopoly over the labor market. Competition in that area - where workers can work for less than minimum wage if they choose - will make the unions redundant. Likewise, the National Party is only looking after the interests of its constituency, Australian farmers - who believe (like farmers in France, America and Japan) that farming is a lifestyle, and not a business, and that the world owes them a living. The idea of putting agriculture on a market basis terrifies them, and rightfully so. Both groups - the blue-collar trade unionists, and the farmers - claim that their interests are the interests of Australia as a whole. But this is false. Non-white immigration does more damage to Australia than free trade or privatization (in my opinion), but historically the unions and the farmers have done little to oppose it. A few trade unionists in Australia are now speaking out against immigration, simply because present government policies have loopholes which allow immigrants to work for below minimum wage. But, obviously, the concern of these unionists is based on self-interest, nothing more.

And if we are to judge the rightness or wrongness of every economic policy by self-interest, very well then: competition and privatization does little to hurt me as a person. For example, competition in the airline industry in Australia has allowed cut-price airlines like Jetstar and Virgin Blue to appear, which allow me to travel to nationalist conferences at cut-rate prices - something which would be impossible a few decades ago when established monopoly-protected airlines like Quantas dominated the market.

The problem is, I think, that many nationalists in Australia are prone to adopt the farmers' and the unions' struggles as their own; likewise, nationalists in other Western countries elsewhere do the same - champion the interests of farmers, or unions, or local business, against competition, from within or without.

They do so reflexively, because, they feel that, by being nationalist, they must side with the Left on nearly every economic issue. In my own experience, every nationalist I have encountered has opposed the neoliberal agenda of free trade, privatization, deregulation, union-busting, etc. Nationalists take a left-wing position on most economic issues. This is for a number of reasons; but I think that the main cause is that the nationalism of Europe in the 1930s and 1940s was economically on the Left, and that that period of nationalism still has a great ideological influence on Western nationalists today.

And I agree: nationalism is, and should remain, Left when it comes to the economy. But groups like local manufacturers, unions and farmers are very strong already, and do not need the support of nationalists; furthermore, they will reject any overtures we will care to make towards them, either because they do not give a damn about the issues we care about - e.g., immigration, or freedom of speech - or because they do not want to offend Jews and liberals.

Besides which, by focusing on free trade, or privatization, or competition, we are ignoring the real issues. For instance, we are not paying attention to the problem of the massive unemployment which exists in most Western countries. We in Australia have quite a severe unemployment problem - something which may come as a surprise to foreign readers, as the official rate is only 4.6%. But other statistics belie that figure. We have, in Australia, 2.6 million Australians on welfare. Of that 2.6 million, 700,000 are on the disability pension.

We also have an epidemic of single parents, most of them women, collecting single parents' pension: 423,000 as of September 2006.

Around 250,000 men in Australia between the ages of 25 and 44 are not looking for work.

So why is the unemployment rate only 4.6%? Firstly, because people are only counted as looking for work (and therefore being unemployed) if they are willing to take up a job in one week's time; secondly, anyone working at least two hours a week is counted as being employed full-time. These methods for counting the unemployed are set by the International Labor Organization, an agency of the United Nations, and have been used in Australia since 1978. (Previously, the method used was to count the number of people on unemployment benefit. If that method were still in use today, the official unemployment rate would be 5.4%). Most other countries in the world use this method as well.

Understandably, that ILO method can downplay the number of unemployed quite dramatically. But hardly any mainstream political figure in Australia, whether on the Right or Left, questions its use; after all, the figures it produces are just too good. The conservative politicians, who have never been unemployed or experienced any significant economic hardship, simply assume that the figures are correct and that the present conservative government has created a jobs cornucopia. (And indeed, deregulation of the labor market since the 1990s has created plenty of two hour a week jobs). So their welfare policy is fairly simple: the unemployed are scum, and deserve to be treated as such; the best policy is to use psychological pressure to force them off benefits and get them to look for work.

The policy has been successful insofar as that it has forced many people off unemployment benefits. It is safe to assume that many unemployed (or women, for instance, who otherwise would have been unemployed) have jumped ship and become disabled or single parents, simply because the requirements for those two pensions are less strict.

From my own experience (and the experience of anyone who is an urban commuter, or spends time in the central business districts of Australia's major cities), there is a growing, almost ubiquitous, Australian underclass. (The characteristics of an 'underclass' are, following the American author Charles Murray's definition, are: low rates of participation in the labor force, low educational attainment, a record of petty crime, chronic drug and alcohol abuse, poor diet, anti-social behavior, and a penchant for giving birth to children out of wedlock). Comprising the underclass are a small, but growing percentage of the white population and a large percentage of the Indigenous population. Underclass people cannot find employment for two reasons: there are not enough low-wage, low-skill jobs for them, and employers find them too obnoxious and unprofessional to hire them anyway (at least at prevailing wage rates).

In Hitler's Germany, as we know, full employment prevailed. A small underclass existed (as it does in every society) which led a dissolute lifestyle and refused to work. The German government's policy was to offer a long-term unemployed person a job, and if that person refused a job offer three times in a row, they ended up in a concentration camp and wore a uniform with a black triangle - the symbol for 'asocial' prisoners.

In general, such a policy can be justified - in a situation of full employment. But Australia is not such a full-employment economy, even though the liberal democratic politicians say otherwise. The same can be said for other Western countries. (It is hard to judge the unemployment levels in other countries from a distance; but we can say for certain that unemployment in France and Germany is high, and that the same is true for most countries in Europe. Britain, which has low official unemployment figures, has a large number of people subsisting off the welfare state, as do the Scandinavian countries).

As to why we have a growing underclass, a number of complex social and economic explanations exist.

For one, most of the underclass traditionally would work in low-wage, low-skill jobs. But minimum wage laws effectively cancel out any such jobs. As well as that, most of the underclass are drop-outs from the working classes, who traditionally worked in low-skill manufacturing jobs, which are now being relocated offshore in Third World countries because of, among other things, minimum wage laws, high taxes and the simple fact that most workers in the Third World have a lower standard of living and therefore will demand lower wages than Australians.

Besides the economic, there are underlying social causes. The American author mentioned before, Charles Murray, believes that the decline of the institution of marriage is responsible for the growth of the underclass. Children in single-parent families grow up without a father who acts as a male role model. That is, the traditional husband and family man - who goes to work every day, stays monogamous, and does not engage in petty crime and anti-social behavior - in the past acted as a role model and a stabilizing influence. Nowadays, the welfare state, with its generous provision of single-parent pensions, pays women to bring up children without fathers. Furthermore, it encourages them to have more children in order to collect more money.

All of these explanations have value, I believe; even the work of a mainstream conservative like Murray has value in that it goes a long way to explaining the growth of the underclass, and what needs to be done about it. But it is essential for nationalists to recognize that nothing can be done about the underclass problem, and the unemployment problem, in a mainstream liberal democracy. Because of its inefficiencies, liberal democracy can do little to alleviate social and economic problems in the West - merely stave them off. (For instance, the German government has had 16 years to do something about Germany's unemployment problem, but has failed, and failed miserably, and will continue to fail).

But we have to draw a distinction here between the underclass and the rest: there are many people in Australia, and in the Western countries, who are down on their luck and who are not underclass scum. These people have been trampled on by successive liberal democratic governments. They have been left behind by both the mainstream Right and Left because, among other things, the unemployment statistics say they do not exist. (In Australia there is the spectacle of the person who is over fifty-five and who is without work. No employer will hire them because of their age, and, at the same time, they are too young to collect the old-age pension. There are also large numbers of over-educated university students who graduate every year and who are destined to dead-end and insecure casual work, or work as security guards, taxi drivers, etc. Also, a number of students who are still studying are forced to rely on charity thanks to, among other things, government cuts and the abolition of student services previously funded by the government).

It is my opinion that these people are potential recruits for nationalism - and good recruits at that. For one, they have some education and are (unlike the underclass) fundamentally decent people; secondly, they have the potential intelligence and perceptiveness to see that their problems will not be solved by a change in government at the ballot box. They will be receptive to the nationalist argument that the structural deficiencies in the economies of the West, and particularly the Western welfare-state countries like Australia, France and Germany, are due to the deficiencies inherent in liberal democracy.

So what are the solutions for the West's economic problems, in particular, its unemployment (and underemployment) problems? I am not arguing for complete and total socialism - as it exists in Cuba and North Korea - and I am not arguing for the complete cessation of 'free-market reform' either: only that there has to be a medium between the two. But the right direction lies towards the Left and not to the Right. We need to move towards an economy where people are treated on the basis of their 'merit', their 'social value', and not merely their market value. There are plenty of decent people who have been ground under by the economic mill, and who deserve better treatment.

In a previous article published - The radicalization of the middle classes - it was argued that nationalism should aim at forming its base in the middle class, following the example of the National Socialist and fascist movements of the 1920s and 1930s. That recommendation is correct: but it is essential to point out that the middle-class followers of

Italian Fascism and National Socialism - the office workers, the small business owners, the intellectuals - were, for the most part, unemployed (or underemployed). They understood, instinctively, that the fascists were acting in their interest. Hitler never said anything as blunt as, 'Vote for me, German office girls, and I'll get you a job'; but that was the underlying message in the National Socialists speeches and writings. National Socialist and Italian Fascist propaganda was pitched at a fairly high intellectual level, aimed at Germans and Italians (and other Europeans) with a degree of education. That, combined with the repeated emphasis in that propaganda on 'social' needs and 'social' justice, meant that the lower middle-classes recognized fascism for what it was: socialism in their interest, and not that of the working-classes (who were either attracted to communism or mainstream social democracy).

Circumstances today, of course, are different than from Europe and the rest of the West in the 1930s. But they are similar in that the times are ripe for social revolution - a revolution of the decent, i.e., people who are not underclass but who deserve better treatment. The likes of a Hayek may object to such 'subjective' assessments of value. But governments are always allocating resources on the basis of some perceived merit, and this is a fact of life. In Australia, for instance, immigrants from Sudan get preferential treatment; waves of Africans are brought over, either to work in low-wage, low-skill jobs, or, more likely, put on welfare with that last wave of 'refugees' we all had to feel sorry for - the Vietnamese. Whatever contribution the African, Vietnamese and Muslim immigrants make to economic life (and it is minimal, in my opinion) is overshadowed by the social cost. (But, to Hayek, we cannot assess 'social' cost).

Nationalists will have, in my view, little to no serious competition when it comes to tackling the 'social question'. The Marxists, surprisingly enough, are out of touch on social issues. In the main, this is because of their narrow-minded ideology. In their worldview, there are only 'good' working-class people and 'bad' corporations (with the petit bourgeoisie existing in the middle). The Marxist fights for social justice for the working-class, but ignores the plight of the middle-class. Furthermore, the analysis of the Marxists is limited: social problems are caused by capitalism and the big corporations; the idea that Jews, for instance, could be a contributing factor to social decadence and decline is nonsense - anti-Semitism is 'the socialism of fools'. The Marxists further alienate themselves from ordinary people of Indo-European descent when they champion the rights of immigrants, and denounce any opposition to immigration as racism, fascism, etc.

As we all know, the economic depression of the 1930s brought the German National Socialists to power. Many Westerners believed that fascism was a viable alternative to liberal democracy, which, it was perceived, had failed. It is for that reason that more than a few nationalists today express a desire for some economic catastrophe, comparable on a scale to that of the 1930s, to occur. After all, that will only increase support for nationalism. (We know that, electorally, the German National Socialists did badly in the late 1920s because, among other things, of the improving economy). But I believe that this argument is fallacious. For one thing, the catastrophe, in many Western countries, is already here. Germany today, for instance, has more people on its unemployment rolls than during the Depression.

In order to attract more public support, nationalists need to bring up, again and again, the 'social question' - and persuade people that the causes of any economic deprivation go deeper than the mainstream analysis. (That is, we know that the economies of the West may be bad because of high inflation, high interest rates, high taxes; but why the high interest rates, why the high taxes? Why do we have a class of politicians who embark on policies which we all know will only hurt the economy?).

At the same time, we must not make the mistake of leaping straight into electoral politics, expecting that, once we form a new, populist party, nationalists will come to power and make everything right again. Pauline Hanson's One Nation did a good job, initially, of addressing the 'social question' and the concerns of people who had been left behind by the policies of the mainstream parties; but it failed to build up a critical mass of popular support as preparation for any electoral activity. At the federal elections of 1998, One Nation received one million votes, but failed to break through Australia's proportional voting system; the major parties triumphed.

Nationalism must, before it becomes embodied in a party, be a state of mind and a mass movement; a state of mind and a movement which exists in a large segment of the population - the 'decent' we have identified here.

6

AGAINST PRESS FREEDOM: ERNST ZÜNDEL AND PARLIAMENTARISM

As most readers know, the Holocaust revisionist Ernst Zündel was sentenced to five years jail by a German court - after being kidnapped, from America to Canada, held for two years without charge in a Canadian prison (under anti-terrorist legislation) and then deported to Germany, where he was charged with multiple counts of Holocaust denial. It is unknown, at this point, if the court will take into account time served. Predictably, the German media were hostile to Zündel and his defense team, but worried if the severity of the sentence - and the fact that freedom of speech on the Holocaust is illegal in Germany and around 30 states in Europe - would turn the 'Neo-Nazi' Zündel into a martyr.

The intention of this article is to look at the question of freedom of the press, and freedom of speech, in nationalist ideology, in relation to cases like Zündel's. The repression of Holocaust revisionists and nationalists in the West is denounced, by nationalist activists, as being a violation of those two freedoms. Liberal democracies claim to be that - liberal - but, at the same time, censure and punish denials of the Holocaust, as well as expressions of racism. The hypocrisy of this position is pointed out by nationalists. While I agree that it is a contradiction, certainly, my argument here is to defend the likes of Zündel on different grounds from the liberal. That is, because our opponents are themselves illiberal, we do not need to become liberals in opposition to them.

I am unwilling to criticize the revisionists - who have suffered for their ideals, in the cause of both truth and nationalism - and their followers. But it must be said that their work suffers from an ideological deficiency, even an emptiness. Zündel, Rudolf, Graf, Faurisson and others write on contemporary political events, with great insight, not the least because of their experiences. But their politics, fundamentally, boils down to the view that once the truth about the Holocaust is revealed, the West, and the rest of the world oppressed by Zionism (or those acting as proxies for Zionism, e.g., the Americans in Iraq and Afghanistan), will be free. It is, in fact, liberalism (as will be explained later). There is a lack of an intellectual, and even an ideological, basis in their writings. This is ironic, given that the revisionists are accused by Jews as being part of a vast 'Neo-Nazi' underground, a conspiracy to introduce a 'Fourth Reich', and, by the peculiar Jewish logic, of justifying a future slaughter of the Jews by denying a past one. If any of these accusations were true, revisionism would be part of a political movement, and revisionists would be acting with a political intent. But it is the lack of a theoretical basis, leading to political action, which is a source of weakness in Holocaust revisionism, and much of contemporary Western nationalism.

The absence of an ideological center, in Holocaust revisionism and in unreflective nationalism, means that both become easy prey for other, consistent, intellectually-worked ideologies. That is, because the Holocaust revisionist lacks an ideological center and ideological training, he will take on board the first ideological system that comes along, and spout its values. Hence the adoption of liberal rhetoric among the revisionists and the activists who support them: free speech is concomitant with democracy, we cannot have a liberal society without debate, etc. Just as the uneducated trade unionist will take up Marxist rhetoric and Marxist slogans, the revisionists take up liberalism, and nationalist activists are in perpetual danger of becoming liberals.

In the case of the trade unionist, Marxism does no harm; in the case of the nationalist, liberalism does a great deal of harm. For, in my opinion, liberalism is the source of all the problems which bedevil the nationalist so much: immigration, Zionism, the repression of Holocaust revisionism, bad economic policy and a host of other evils which are the product of, simply put, bad government. It is not that liberal ideology is a direct cause of, say, the repression of Holocaust revisionism; only that the adoption of a liberal political system will invariably lead to negative consequences, such as that repression.

In this instance, the work of Carl Schmitt is useful, in particular, his book, The Crisis of Parliamentary Democracy (1923). The second chapter in that book - 'The principles of parliamentarism' - outlines the ideology of what Schmitt calls 'parliamentarism'. He expounds the view that parliamentarism is an offshoot of liberalism, which is itself a complete view of the world, a weltanschauung, even a metaphysical system (no matter what its proponents say). Liberalism sees the world as being made up of free and independent individuals. In the economic sphere, these individuals compete with one another in the market, selling their goods and services. The individual who is most successful - that is, who earns the most patronage from the consumer - wins. Even though some individuals lose out in the struggle, overall, the clash of competing interests leads to a greater harmony, a greater equilibrium, a greater balance.

Does liberalism apply in the purely political sphere, outside of the marketplace? The answer, says Schmitt, is yes. Parliament is itself an instance of this clash of individual wills which, in the end, leads to equilibrium. But the contest is not a market one: it is a contest of ideas. The essence of political liberalism is free and open discussion of ideas and opinions between free and independent individuals, and the willingness of those individuals to be persuaded. From that debate, the 'truth' emerges - truth emerges from the great debate, the never-ending discussion that takes place in parliament.

Following the French thinker Guizot, Schmitt lists three characteristics of the parliamentarist system:

(1) *that "the powers" are always forced to discuss and thereby seek the truth together; (2) that the openness of the whole of political life places "the powers" under the citizens' control; and (3) that press freedom prompts citizens to seek the truth for themselves and to make it known to "the powers". Parliament is accordingly the place in which particles of reason that are strewn unequally among human beings gather themselves*

and bring public power under control. (Carl Schmitt, The Crisis of Parliamentary Democracy, p. 35).

He adds, *'Freedom of speech, freedom of press, freedom of assembly, freedom of discussion, are.. really life-and-death questions for liberalism'* (p. 36).

The rationale behind the secret ballot is that one's voting choices must remain private - that is, they are the expression of a private, free individual. Again, from conflicting individual interests, conflicting private opinions, a harmony, a balance, emerges. Through voting, the people find truth - or rather, they elect representatives who find truth for them through open debate in parliament. (Schmitt notes - and this is an important point - that democracy does not necessarily depend on the practice of elections. The sum of voters is not the sum of the people).

Liberalism and parliamentarism are the source of the structure of our modern political system. For instance, the concept of the separation of powers, or the division (or balance) of powers, in the representative assemblies, finds its justification in liberalism. That the American legislature, executive and judiciary should be made up of individuals from different parties is seen as good by the liberal media: it represents the division of power, in which no single party or institution wields an absolute total of power. And that the same divisions repeat themselves, not only at the American federal, but at the state level - at the level of the state executive, legislature and judiciary - is praiseworthy. Why? Because the multiplicity of opinions, the clash of opinions in a free and open discussion is taking place at every level.

Parliament becomes a forum for debate, for clashing opinions, for free and open discussion - and for finding the truth. The rules of the game are that every participant in the debate respects one another: that the other participant has the right to speak, and speak freely, because this is the only way that truth can emerge. A participant with a 'totalizing' truth - for instance, the Marxist, who believes that truth has already been arrived at in the works of Lenin and Trotsky, and not through debate - is not welcome. Or, if he is to be allowed into the parliament, he must agree to respect the rules.

One can see, from this, how important a free press is. It provides another venue for free and open discussion. As well as that, through publicity, it reveals truth. Free reporting exposes secret government business (or secret corporate business) to the glare of publicity, exposing the truth. Hence the lauding of the work of crusading investigative journalists like Woodward and Bernstein, who exposed to the world the Nixon administration's nefarious doings. The saying that a free press is concomitant to a democracy, to a free and liberal society, has become one of the clichés of our age, if not a dogma, spouted by liberal ideologists and more often by journalists themselves.

We can see that the liberal and parliamentarist doctrine is reflected in the work of the Holocaust revisionists and the activists who fight for them. Holocaust revisionists have a (perhaps naive) view of the value of publicity - that is, the exposure, for all the world to see, of the hoax of the Holocaust shall set the world free. All that would need to be done is for the laws banning Holocaust revisionism in Europe to be repealed, and Europeans would find the truth for themselves. In the calamitous uproar which would follow the revelation of the truth of the Holocaust, the obsessively pro-Zionist, philo-Semitic liberal democratic politicians of Europe, and the West, would be forced to recognize the error of their ways. This view is, in fact, the liberal and parliamentarist view of the value of truth, publicity and the free press.

Likewise, the ultimate justification for Holocaust revisionism - or rather, the right to deny the Holocaust - lies in the liberal doctrine of free speech. If society is made up of free individuals who are to be allowed to express their opinion, in newspaper articles, political demonstrations and in parliamentary debates, then Holocaust revisionists ought to be allowed to do the same. Indeed, the tolerance of Holocaust revisionism is a litmus test for a free society, because many individuals have been conditioned to look at revisionism with revulsion.

So what is wrong with this: what is wrong with using liberal doctrines to justify the practice of Holocaust revisionism? The answer is that liberalism, as a doctrine, is simply false. As Schmitt writes:

Discussion means an exchange of opinion that is governed by the purpose of persuading one's opponent through argument of the truth or justice of something, or allowing oneself to be persuaded of something true or just.... The characteristic of all representative constitutions is that laws arise out of a conflict of opinions (not out of a struggle of interests). To discussion belong shared convictions as premises, the willingness to be persuaded, independence of party ties, freedom from selfish interests. Most people today would regard such disinterestedness as scarcely possible. (Schmitt, Crisis, 'Preface to the second edition (1926)', p.5).

Most of Schmitt's attacks on parliamentarism in this book are in that vein. That is, parliamentarism, or liberalism, does not work the way it should anymore, if it ever did. Parliament is hostage to 'invisible powers', representatives of the unions, big business, the Jewish lobby, and the like - and those representatives are not, for one, willing to be persuaded. The real government business - like the kidnapping, deportation of Ernst Zündel, and even the outcome of his trial - is done behind closed doors.

One can still uphold parliamentarism as the best system, the best available at the present time. But if that is all we have as a justification for a system - that the only justification we have for it is a purely pragmatic one, that we should keep it simply because it continues to work, and work well - then that system is lost, and we can no longer believe in its validity. (Schmitt compares the present loss of belief in parliamentarism to the waning away of the belief in the divine right of kings).

But the implications of a lack of belief in the value of parliamentarism are manifold. For one, the institutions of parliament - freedom and speech and immunity for parliamentary representatives, the openness of parliamentary proceedings, the declassification of cabinet minutes after thirty years, the Freedom of Information Act and so on - lose their meaning. And likewise, liberal beliefs, practices and institutions - the separation of powers, the value of balance of conflicting opinions and interests, and all the other legal and constitutional traits of a liberal order (which have been described in Schmitt's book but not been detailed here) - lose their meaning. So the effect of Schmitt's criticisms (and the criticisms of other opponents of liberal parliamentarism, i.e., communist groups) is that the sacred cows of our present system of liberal democracy - free and fair elections, parliament and parliamentary procedures, free press and free speech - lose their sacred qualities.

Many nationalists feel this already, of course. They feel, for instance, that the liberal media in the West is not so liberal - that it is in the service of 'hidden powers'. The Australian publicly-owned broadcasting TV channel SBS, for instance, failed to mention the Zündel sentencing on the day that it occurred, choosing instead to focus on the death of a minor Vichy-era French official who may or may not have been responsible for sending thousands of French Jews to Auschwitz for gassing and cremation. The entire Western media constantly keeps the atrocities of the Germans in WWII (real or alleged) in the public eye, around the clock, and is not even interested in ideological balance. (For instance, the death of an American soldier who worked as a guard at one of Eisenhower's death camps in occupied France, or a Polish communist official who oversaw the ethnic cleansing of millions of Germans, would hardly be remarked upon).

But this applies in other areas of political reporting as well. Take, for instance, the press' uniform acceptance of the Bush administration's contention that Bin Laden and Al Qaeda were responsible for 9/11; or Bush's declaration of 'victory' three weeks into the Iraq war; or that it was Saddam Hussein who had been 'captured hiding' in an abandoned farm house in Tikrit. In each of these cases (and many others), some real investigative reporting, or at least some questioning of the official line, was called for. Had the Americans really conquered Iraq in three weeks? Was the man the Americans claimed to have 'captured' really Saddam Hussein? Did Bin Laden really carry out 9/11? Are the daily communiqués from 'Al Qaeda' genuine, or the product of a Western intelligence agency? Perhaps, in each of these cases, the Bush administration could have been exposed to the unpleasant glare of publicity, the truth could have been made known to the masses, a la Woodward and Bernstein. But no. The truth is that the Western media is equally as totalitarian, and supine before State power, as much as the Chinese or North Korean media is. And the same can be said, by extension, for academia, the entertainment industry. All seem to be under the same central control, or at least, subscribing to the same ideology. Even the self-professed alternatives to that mainstream ideology - for instance, Noam Chomsky, or Michael Moore - strenuously deny, or refuse to mention, the existence of a Jewish lobby in the United States which influences the latter's foreign policy in the Middle East (hence, the radical Chomsky is allotted front-page space in the Guardian newspaper).

All of this is well-known to nationalists: our lack of belief in the freedom of press is as pronounced as that of the Marxists. The question is what attitude we should take. We can demand, along with those who still believe in liberalism, a truly free press, which gives equal space to Robert Faurisson and a publicist for the Jewish lobby on the same op-ed page; or one can give up on the possibility of there ever being a free press altogether.

I myself subscribe to the latter view. If liberalism, and parliamentarism, has no longer any value, then the concept of a free press no longer has value - it is no longer an ideal we should strive towards. On top of that, the notion of a mainstream Western newspaper ever even considering granting op-ed space to the likes of Faurisson is unlikely - it would take a miracle. Or rather, it would take a cataclysmic revolution in which the Jewish lobby would itself cease to exist as a political force (and hence, there would be no need to grant its agitators 'equal time' in the media).

I am a nationalist before I am a liberal - not a nationalist liberal. My own immediate reaction, on seeing yet another nonsensical Holocaust story on the nightly news, is as follows. Under a nationalist government, all journalists should be made to join a national journalist's union. Membership in that union would require that they refrain from peddling their daily dose of multi-racialist, philo-Semitic, German-hating pap; any journalists who refuse to join will lose their jobs. That system, of managing the news, would be not that different from our existing one, except that such a journalist's union (which, contrary to our hypothetical nationalist one, requires journalists to report constantly on the Holocaust, or denounce the Ku Klux Klan, or denounce apartheid, etc.) is invisible; it has no official existence, although it is constantly making itself felt. The rule is that anything that is untrue - and the Holocaust is untrue - and that anything which is destructive to the long-term survival and health of the Western Christian civilization ought to be suppressed as ruthlessly as any Holocaust revisionism, etc., today is suppressed.

And here we are straying into a grey and murky area. The doctrine that a press should no longer be 'free', that it should serve a political purpose (in our case, a nationalist purpose) - could be anathema to most nationalists. This is because most nationalist and Holocaust revisionist activists are used to being persecuted by the State and its organs. The fact that they receive no help from groups claiming to uphold civil liberties - like Amnesty International, or Human Rights Watch - does not diminish their appetite for liberalism. Indeed, the repression of freedom of speech, in the European countries which ban Holocaust denial, for instance, is held by some nationalist activists to be the manifestation of a new leftist totalitarianism, a new Marxism, which, in the past two decades, has seized power through social democratic and communist parties and hence undermined liberalism and liberal democracy. Many backward-looking Far Right populist parties look nostalgically to the Europe of the 1950s and the 1960s when one could deny the Holocaust with impunity (even in West Germany) and discuss racial and immigration questions openly. So the suggestion that the 'rights' of journalists should be curtailed, that the institution of a 'free press' be attacked, would rankle some nationalists, and understandably so.

But this is, I believe, a misunderstanding of the nationalist ideology. Liberalism's view of freedom is negative: it denies the right of government to interfere in the private sphere of individuals, or at least, seeks to limit that interference to the bare minimum. Many nationalists, unfortunately, only desire that negative freedom: that is, all they want is the freedom to vent their animus against non-white immigrants, indigenous Australians, North American Indians, the Jewish lobbyist, and politically-correct Marxists and multiculturalists - and that is all. Their nationalism cannot be said to be a striving for something: for a better world order, for example, a real improvement in the life of the race they belong to. Their position can be characterized as a reactionary liberalism, a backward-looking liberalism.

Other nationalists, however, do want a better world and do have positive ideals. But, it is argued here, in order to achieve those ideals, it must be recognized that they cannot be achieved in a liberal and parliamentarian political order. The reasons for this are apparent once we examine the tenets of liberalism closely. At the ideological level, liberalism upholds the equality of all human beings: that is, all humans are politically equal simply by virtue of their being adult persons. But an ideology which gives an unskilled, illiterate Mexican immigrant to the United States the same value as a literate, skilled American proletarian or bourgeois is really the antithesis of nationalism; it and nationalism cannot co-exist. Likewise, the parliamentarian system, of selecting leaders and representing the people, is the antithesis of nationalism. Certain policies are popular with the people - for instance, a cessation of non-white immigration, or the reintroduction of the death penalty for child rapists and sex murderers - but parties which uphold such policies are consistently voted down, or never receive the votes they need. This is because, in part, of the voting process itself. The secret ballot system forces voters to think of themselves, not as members of a community, but as private individuals with private economic interests - despite the fact that they are voting on matters of public law which pertains to public matters.

The problem is, in part, a procedural, and a legal and constitutional one. It is no good having political ideals if the means of bringing them into reality - parliamentarism - is flawed. The ideals of nationalism - a positive nationalism - are, at bottom, not so complicated. The nationalist, in the last analysis, wants a community with a high standard of living, safe and pleasant cities and towns to live and work, a healthy and uplifting cultural life, a society in which ugliness and squalor are removed, a community where the members feel a sense of belonging with one another and care for one another while at the same time respecting one another's autonomy. These values are not so controversial, and even liberal democratic politicians would agree that they are desirable. The main difference between the nationalist, and the believer in mainstream liberal democracy, is that the latter believes that goals such as civic cleanliness and safety, and an increase in the standard of living, can be achieved alongside, for example, massive non-white immigration and the abolition of the death penalty. Hence the absurd spectacle of the social democratic, left-liberal politician who advocates an increase funding for the arts and better urban planning while, at the same time, advocating policies which increase squalor and ugliness. (In Sydney, Australians are faced with the irony of having the Sydney Opera House - a famous and distinctive Australian cultural monument - located a few meters away from an enclave of homeless heroin addicts. The urban centre of Sydney is itself populated with an enormous number of Asian immigrants who certainly feel no connection, no sense of cultural kinship, with the Western culture which produces the operas and ballets performed at the Opera House, and neither can the abusive, drunken, uneducated Aboriginals who live in nearby suburbs).

Why is this? The answer, in this case, is that the social democrat is a socialist, and a believer in the power of government to improve the standard of living of its citizens - economically, socially, culturally. But, at the same time, he is a liberal: individuals should be allowed to do what they want, so long as they are not breaking the law. Drunken Aboriginals, the homeless heroin addicts, the beggars in our urban centers, non-white immigrants, all have rights - as does the film-maker who glorifies interracial couplings. Child rapists may have broken the law, but even they must be supported, at the taxpayer's expense, for the rest of their lives in jail instead of being executed - for execution would be inhumane. And so it goes. Social democracy, because of its subscription to parliamentarism (the 'democracy' in 'social democracy') , invariably ends up removing government policy of any common sense and decency, and making day to day living, especially in the cities, uglier and harder.

So the answer is: in order to achieve nationalist goals, the existing liberal and parliamentarian order must be overturned. We must stop pretending that we are liberals, no matter how attractive some of its ideals may seem. I myself have been to nationalist conferences which have come under attack from both political authorities and anti-racist activists. Commonly, participants will defend the right of that conference take place in the name of the liberal right of freedom of speech. Such sloganeering has real power, undoubtedly. But we nationalists must ask ourselves: are we nationalists undertaking such events in the name of freedom and liberalism, or because we seek to improve the lives of the fellow members of our community, our nation? The question answers itself.

German media commentators often call for the banning of German nationalist organizations like the NPD in the name of 'democracy' (i.e., liberal democracy). They claim that, while the likes of the NPD demand the protection of their rights as a political organization in the name of liberalism, they are opposed to liberalism. (They would oppose the freedom of Turkish immigrants to live in Germany, for example). So, paradoxically, the German liberal democratic State must be illiberal to be liberal, and ban the German nationalist groups and wipe them out.

Those commentators are right, in one respect: liberalism and nationalism are ultimately incompatible (although nationalism and democracy are not, as Schmitt argues in his book). In the end, one must go. Nationalists cannot, in Germany, for example, agitate against 'democracy' directly - that is forbidden under law. (Probably, 'democracy' could be agitated against in Germany, but that would require a lawyer's knowledge of the German constitution. In any case, the defenders of 'liberal democracy' can always twist a constitution to say whatever they want). But the works of Carl Schmitt, for example, are still legal in countries like Germany which have 'anti-anti-democratic' laws. Liberalism, and parliamentarism, can still be assaulted intellectually, and that is where we must begin.

7

THE MYTH OF DEMOCRACY

I. Introduction

I often discuss nationalist politics with non-nationalist friends. Usually, it transpires that they are in agreement with me on certain issues which we nationalists are concerned with. But, while they do end up agreeing with me, they often note that nationalism seems to lack a centre; that it does not seem to be a coherent ideology moving towards a fixed goal. While I am reluctant to admit it in front of them, I am forced to concede that they are right. The reason is, I think, as follows. Nationalists are often categorized as 'extreme'; but, while I agree that nationalist must be, in the end, extreme, there is a difference between the extremist ideology of today's nationalism and the extremist ideologies of the recent past - fascism and communism, for a start. The latter ideologies moved towards a goal, and subordinated all their activities towards that goal. In the case of fascism, the brownshirts and blackshirts aimed at little more than bringing their Führer or their Duce to power, through a combination of legal and extra-parliamentary means; for the communists, to bring achieve the dictatorship of the proletariat, again through the same combination. Both had clear-cut political goals. But the nationalists of today are moving towards - what, exactly?

We are mostly agreed on what we want: a cessation of non-white immigration, and so on. But we are not united on how to get there. This leads to frustration amongst the nationalist activists; and that frustration, in turn, can lead to a desire for violence - which explains, in part, the attraction so many nationalists have for the violent creed of William Pierce's The Turner Diaries.

Here, in this article, I am sketching out a path - a political path - which nationalists can use to reach the end goals we all agree upon. But, in order to travel upon it, we will have to change our thinking, and give up certain of the old political dogmas which we have gotten used to. Living in liberal democracies, we have become accustomed to certain liberal political institutions: free elections, the secret ballot, the separation of powers, the multi-party system, federalism, and certain liberal freedoms - freedom of association, freedom of assembly, and freedom of the press. We in the West find it hard to imagine a world without these institutions, and are trained, by the media, to look disparagingly at countries which do not have them (the former Rhodesia, Thailand, the Middle East, all of North and Sub-Saharan Africa). So nationalists are inclined to take them for granted, and even regard them as desirable. But it is these liberal institutions which are, in my view, holding nationalism back from achieving victory - these and nothing else.

So, in this article, I aim at breaking down traditional thinking on these matters of politics. I will first give an account of Carl Schmitt's notion of democracy, in an attempt to show how democracy can be at the basis of a nationalist, and even authoritarian, government. I will then look at Schmitt's ideas concerning dictatorship and constitutions, particularly in the context of German political history during and after the Weimar republic, up to the present day. Finally, I will give a few arguments against liberal democracy and liberal freedoms, and make some suggestions on how nationalists are to achieve political power, using some examples from recent political history.

II. Is democracy nationalist?

Both Alain De Benoist and Tomislav Sunic have written on democracy and Carl Schmitt's interpretation of the concept. Both agree that, by Schmitt's definition, democracy is, surprisingly enough, not anti-nationalist. According to Schmitt, democracy is not elections, and is not liberal parliamentarism and all the associated liberal freedoms: freedom of the press, freedom of assembly, speech, association, and so on. A distinction is to be drawn between democracy on one hand and liberalism on the other (Schmitt made that distinction, most famously, in his The Crisis of Parliamentary Democracy (1923)).

Democracy is, in Schmitt's view, a statement of identity. The simple definition of democracy is the rule of the majority. That definition, says Schmitt, implies that the members of that majority are identical to one another in some way, that is, that they hold some property in common, whether it be race, religion, ethnicity, or some quality - Britishness, Australian-ness. Democracy requires homogeneity. And the sharing of that property, which leads to homogeneity, means that the sharers are politically equal.

As an example of democracy, Schmitt gives the examples of the ancient Greek city states of Athens and Sparta. Members of Spartan or Athenian democracy were equal to one another in possessing the virtue of a Spartan or Athenian citizenship. But a group within that democracy - the slave caste - were unequal, not possessing full political rights. So, at the root of democracy is the equality of equals (who make up the democratic majority) and the inequality of unequals (who make up the democratic minority).

Schmitt gives, as another example, the British Empire: did the 300 million citizens of the Empire possess the same rights, i.e., were they as equal as Britons? Clearly, no: the citizens of the United Kingdom possessed political rights denied to others in the Commonwealth. Schmitt also cites Australia, and in particular, the application of the White Australia policy. Immigrants who were not white were to be excluded from Australian democracy, and all the benefits of Australian citizenship that come from being one of the majority, the 'equal equals'.

It may seem, from the last example, that when Schmitt talks of homogeneity, he is talking of a racial homogeneity. But this is not necessarily the case. Some of the member nations of the British Commonwealth - Canada, New Zealand, Australia, South Africa - were white, and yet not sharing the same rights as Britons. Likewise, it is uncertain whether or not the distinction between 'slave' and 'citizen' in the ancient world was a racial one - whether or not the Spartans were white and the Helots were non-white. And, on Schmitt's definition, one could construct the idea of an Islamic democracy, where all the equal citizens are alike in that they are Muslim. One can also point out that the Jewish democracy - Israel - has members who are alike in their Jewishness (but not their race). (And, like a true, Schmittian democracy, Israel denies certain political rights to non-citizens - in particular, the non-Jewish Arab citizens, and the Palestinians in the Occupied Territories).

Schmitt's notion of democratic equality stands in contrast to that of the liberal - for the liberal believes that all people, whether members of a democracy or no, are equal by virtue of being adult persons. Liberalism believes in a radical egalitarianism. In a truly liberal world, all distinctions between citizens and non-citizens in democracies, or equals and unequals, would be abolished. So, rightfully understood, democracy is the enemy of liberalism: the concept of 'liberal democracy' contains two contradictory creeds - liberalism and democracy - which threaten to tear it apart. Hence, 'the crisis of parliamentary democracy'.

If we are to take Schmitt's definition of democracy on board, we can see that immigration - massive non-white immigration - threatens American democracy. In fact, American democracy, in the past fifty years, has suffered two blows. The first was desegregation of Afro-Americans in the 1950s and 1960s; the other was massive Hispanic immigration from the 1990s onwards. Before the desegregation period, America could be said to be a democracy in Schmitt's sense: its citizens - of European descent - were equal, its Afro-Americans unequal, denied full political rights of American citizenship. But, after de-segregation, America moved towards a liberal (non-democratic) equality: Americans and Afro-Americans were equal simply on the basis of their being adult persons. Now the same, anti-democratic process is occurring with the apportioning of political rights to the massive numbers of Hispanic immigrants, legal or illegal.

III. Democracy, constitutions, dictatorship

The other innovation of Schmitt's theory was that it pointed out that democracy need not necessarily be liberal-democratic. Dictatorship - whether it be Marx's 'dictatorship of the proletariat', or the dictatorship of fascism - could be democratic. Influenced by Schmitt on this point, Yockey writes, in the chapter called 'Democracy' in Imperium, that 'In Spanish South America, where the money power was not absolute, a whole tradition of democratic dictators— Bolivar, Rosas, Francia, O'Higgins, some of the best known— show the powerful authoritarian tendency in popular government'. Which explains why movements like German National Socialism and Italian Fascism could be, paradoxically, democratic (in terms of their following among the majority of the German and Italian people respectively) and at the same time hierarchical, illiberal and dictatorial. A regime which forbids elections, or the formation of opposing political parties, need not necessarily lack popular support of the democratic majority. Indeed, the populace, says Schmitt, can give it support through 'acclamation', and passive consent.

I think I have made the case, then, for seeing nationalism as a democratic project: nationalist activists could be said to represent the best tendencies of American, French, German, Australian, British, etc., democracy. (This is one reason why the NPD calls itself the 'National Democratic Party of Germany').

In this context, it is worthwhile to give an account of Schmitt's political career, and political positions, to see the relevance of his thinking to the national struggle today. Schmitt, as a constitutional lawyer, was engrossed for most of his career with the analysis of constitutions. (By 'constitution', I do not mean merely the written constitutions of a state, but its makeup, its political structure, its genotype). For most of his early work, he was fascinated by the concept of the political 'exception' - a state of unlimited power, and the complete suspension, if not overturning, of the existing constitutional order.

By 'exception', he is really referring to dictatorship. In the popular mind, a dictatorship is a regime run by a tyrant, a despot, who is usually a little man in a military uniform laden with medals and who has megalomaniacal tendencies. But, in the strict, juridical definition of the term, a dictatorship is something which occurs when the division between the separation of powers is broken down - when the executive takes up the powers of the legislature and the judiciary. In a liberal state - which stipulates a separation of powers - this entails the amending, or even the destruction, of the existing constitutional order. (An amendment of a written constitution is no easy thing to achieve: in Australia, it requires a referendum which will deliver a majority of votes in the majority of electorates in a majority of states - which explains why, out of 44 proposals to amend the Australian constitution, only eight have been approved). Schmitt calls the subject, the possessor of the power to destroy and create constitutions, the pouvoir constituant.

Schmitt liked to make the distinction between two kinds of dictatorship: the sovereign and the commissarial. The sovereign dictator suspends the separation of powers with the intention of exercising pouvoir constituant, of making a new constitutional order: an example of this is Marx's revolutionary 'dictatorship of the proletariat'. The commissarial dictator, on the other hand, acts on a more limited basis. He intervenes, temporarily, in political life, suspending parts of the constitutional order and takes upon himself extraordinary powers - i.e., abrogating the legislative and even the judiciary functions to himself and ruling by decree (bills not voted upon by the legislature). An example of this is the period of the Indian Emergency from 1975 to 1977, when Prime Minister Indira Ghandi suspended parts of the constitution and ruled by decree.

The commissarial dictatorship is only temporary: after the period of the 'exception', as Schmitt puts it, expires, it is expected that the normal state of affairs will resume. As Evola writes, in Men Among the Ruins (chapter two, 'Sovereignty - Authority - Imperium'), 'In the best period of the Roman civilization, the dictatorship was conceived and allowed as a temporary remedy; far from replacing the existing order, it was its reintegration'.

In the Weimar constitution, Reichspräsident Hindenburg acted as commissarial dictator. Under article 48, Hindenburg could suspend parts of the constitution (including liberal rights guaranteed under the constitution, e.g., freedom of press, freedom of assembly, freedom of association) and pass laws without votes from the legislature. This state of affairs was only temporary: if it were not, the Weimar constitution would not be based on democratic sovereignty - the sovereignty of the German people - but on the sovereignty of the Reichspräsident, who would be acting as monarch, or Führer. Power, under the rules of the constitution, was to be passed back to the people.

During the 1920s and early 1930s, Schmitt placed great hope in Hindenburg and article 48. To him, the office of Reichspräsident, and the German army and bureaucracy, represented the true German State - a 'nation bearing stratum', a caste of national leaders standing above liberal-democratic, party-politics. Schmitt decried the practice of the communists, National Socialists, Catholic and other Weimar-era parties, of politicising every part of civil life - by forming politicized kindergardens, youth groups, women's groups, trade unions, teacher's groups, lawyer's groups, doctor's groups and the like. Schmitt called this 'quantitative' politics: the intrusion of the party-political sphere into civil society and every part of the State. This 'partyfication' of German life was to be resisted, in his view, because it took power away from the German State, making it subject to democratic demands. The excess of democracy, he felt, explained the failures of the parliamentary-liberal system in Weimar - which, more often than not, degenerated into squabbling party and class factions, each aiming for the benefit of their particular group without a view to the good of the whole. He believed that the salvation of Germany lay in conservative chancellors like Papen, and Schleicher, who, with their connections to the military, could steer Germany through political and economic crisis. The role of Reichspräsident Hindenburg was to use the extraordinary powers of article 48 to bypass the squabbling, democratized legislature, when need be.

All that changed with the ascent of Hitler and the NSDAP. In particular, Hitler's famous Enabling Act of March 23, 1933 - 'The law to remedy the distress of the people and the Reich' - gave the executive (Hitler's cabinet) extraordinary powers, including powers to suspend, and rewrite, parts of the Weimar constitution. Schmitt noted that, although the Weimar constitution had not been formally abrogated, the act represented a new, provisional constitution. A sovereign dictatorship had been installed, which was to exercise pouvoir constiuant. Sovereignty had been transferred from the German people to the Führer. After that, Schmitt became a convinced National Socialist and joined the party, now believing that the NSDAP could elevate Germany above democratic, mass-politics and strengthen the German State, which represented the best interests of the German people.

IV. The basic law

We know the sequel to the story, of course. Germany, after being occupied by the Allies, had a new constitution drawn up for it - the Grundgesetz, or Basic Law - and imposed by the Allies by force. Likewise, France and Italy had new constitutions drawn up for them by the Allies as well. Certain 'anti-fascist' provisions were built into the German and Italian constitutions. As students of German political history know, West Germany used article 21 of the Grundgesetz to ban the nationalist Socialist Reich Party in 1952 and the German Communist Party in 1956.

The relevant text, reproduced here for interest, reads:

Article 21

[Political parties]

(1) Political parties shall participate in the formation of the political will of the people. They may be freely established. Their internal

organization must conform to democratic principles. They must publicly account for their assets and for the sources and use of their funds.

(2) Parties that, by reason of their aims or the behavior of their adherents, seek to undermine or abolish the free democratic basic order or to endanger the existence of the Federal Republic of Germany shall be unconstitutional.

The Federal Constitutional Court shall rule on the question of unconstitutionality.

(3) Details shall be regulated by federal laws.

The German government tried to ban the NPD in 2003 using the law, but failed, due to a legal technicality.

The Grundgesetz was conceived as an anti-NSDAP and anti-Weimar constitution. The lawmakers who drafted it knew that certain provisions of the Weimar constitution - like article 48 - allowed Hitler, the chancellor of the Reich, the power to suspend the political, constitutionally-guaranteed rights of his opponents (mainly the communists, but also Social Democrats and conservatives as well) after the event of the Reichstag fire. The emergency powers, granted under article 48, influenced the outcome of the March 5 elections, which, combined with the arrest of Communist Party MPs before the Reichstag sitting, gave Hitler the parliamentary majority needed to amend the constitution and pass the Enabling Act. With the intention of preventing something like that happening again, the Allies made sure that the Grundgesetz would be without emergency powers like article 48. Likewise, other provisions opposed to the spirit of the Weimar and NSDAP constitutions were included. The framers of the Grundgesetz aimed at a) avoiding the instability of Weimar political life and b) preventing a nationalist like Hitler from gaining power legally.

It should be noted, again, that a constitution is much more than a written document: it is the structure, the spirit of a state. The spirit of the German state today is anti-nationalist and anti-"Nazi"; and so, a nationalist organization like the NPD which does not endorse dictatorship (as we have defined it here) is still in danger of being banned under article 21 under a loose interpretation of the letter of the law. And much is the same in other European countries which were under Allied occupation and which had strong nationalist and fascist political movements before and during the war.

So: in Europe, the nationalist parties and organizations are repressed, and are in danger of being banned, because the upholders of the post-war, Allied constitutions detect hidden tendencies in their ideology - hidden tendencies which threaten to undermine the 'free democratic basis' of liberal democratic European states. Now, the question is: does nationalism - inside Europe, and in other Western countries - threaten 'liberal democracy'? Or, if it does not, should it?

V. The nationalist position

The irony is that we nationalists in the non-occupied Western countries have freedom of speech, and can say whatever we want, but choose not to. We can endorse the suspension, or even the overturning, of the existing constitutional order - in Britain, America, Australia, New Zealand - and an end to the separation of powers, but do not do so.

In general, nationalists in the Anglo-Saxon countries take two positions: either they focus, somewhat obsessively, on race, ethnic and cultural issues, and ignore questions of politics (I am thinking here of the American Nutzis, the KKK, Christian Identity, and even certain nationalist intellectuals); or they accept the existing constitutional orders of their respective countries (the Far Right populists). The first position is, on closer examination, the same as the second: it is to accept, and acquiesce, and not challenge, the liberal order.

One cannot blame today's nationalist from wanting to drop out of politics, simply because of the difficulty of nationalists to obtain power through the ballot box. In Australia, for instance, voting is compulsory, and, moreover, based on a system of preferential voting. Both of these devices tend to deliver crushing majorities for the mainstream liberal democratic parties, both at the federal and state level. Minority parties, even with ones with a large measure of support in the community and a large activist base (I am thinking of the Australian Greens, and the Australian Democrats) find it practically impossible to break into the House of Representatives (although finding a Senate seat is somewhat easier). This means that they can never win a majority in the lower house, and so never hold executive power.

This system has its disadvantages and advantages: on the one hand, it delivers stable government, avoiding the instability which occurs, for instance, in modern Italian politics, or in Weimar-era German politics; on the other hand, it prevents nationalists from winning executive power. At the very least, nationalists, along with the Greens and other minority political groups (like the Australian communists), face an uphill battle.

The other reason for political non-involvement on the part of nationalists is, strange as it may seem, an unwillingness to take political responsibility. In this regard, I found a quotation from a book on Schmitt (Carl Schmitt and Authoritarian Liberalism, (1998) by Renato Cristi) illumining:

Schmitt adopts Treitschke's [a 19th century German nationalist thinker] view that 'political romantics' weakened the state by their emphasis on medieval conceptions of social pluralism and communal autonomy. 'Thus everything which German political science had secured during the last century and a half, since Pufendorf had delivered our political thinkers from the yoke of theologians, was once more put into question, and political doctrine was degraded anew to the theocratic conceptions of the Middle Ages... "Corporation, not association" was the catchword of the political romantics, most of whom associated with the term no more than the indefinite conception of a weak state authority, limited by the power of the guilds, diets of nobles, and self-governing communes, and in spiritual matters subjected to the control of the church'. [Cristi, p.74-75.]

It goes without saying that we today are in different circumstances from those described by Treitschke. But there is a similarity between the 'political romantics' of his times and those nationalists who want to shut themselves away, from the world of politics and the world itself, in a racially-homogenous enclave: think of William Pierce and Aryan Nations Pastor Butler in their respective compounds. The tendency exists, as well, outside of America. Indeed, one only has to think of the theories of the great Alain de Benoist, with their emphasis on nationalism restricted to the life of the community, the neighborhood, the corporatist-type association, and their distancing from nationalism in the context of the state (that is, politics). As for the Nutzis, one could expect that the Nutzi groups, particular in America, are working towards a one-party, NSDAP-type state, with a Führer possessing dictatorial powers: but nothing could be further from the truth. Nutzis are content to parade in homemade SA and SS uniforms, and hand out amusing, but crude, fliers denouncing Jews and Negroes. And so it goes.

Let me be clear here: I am not suggesting that we move away from the goal of developing ethnically-homogeneous, separatist communities (which is something de Benoist's theory seems to endorse). What is needed is balance. Schmitt once pointed out that a state and a nation consisted of three things: the people, das Volk; the State and the authorities who are ultimately responsible for political decisions; and the law, administered by bureaucrats, for the day to day running of the state. But nationalism today has become lop-sided, with its obsessive preoccupation with race, race, race - das Volk - to the exclusion of the other political spheres.

As noted before, political activism is hard work; this fact, and the racial-enclave mentality which afflicts a good many modern nationalists, discourages nationalists from entering politics, and studying questions of constitutional law and parliamentary procedure. But there is a notable exception: the Far Right populists - the Pauline Hansons and Le Pens - who have faith in the existing liberal constitutions and electoral systems. They believe their populism is truth and that they represent what the people really think, and so aim to take their truth to parliament, where it will become part of the discussion which is at the heart of liberal political life.

And, in the short term, they can succeed: Hanson's brief time in the Australian federal parliament brought home uncomfortable populist truths to the Australia liberal 'discussing class', that is, the liberal democratic politicians and the journalists. But, in the end, Hanson and her followers had too much faith in the Australian people, the Australian electoral system and the Australian constitution. Her party never achieved the status of a parliamentary faction.

I myself applaud the efforts of the electorally-successful populist parties like the BNP, the FN and the Vlaams Blok; but the existing constitutional order, in Australia, and in Europe, is the disease, not the cure. Take, for instance, one of the pillars of liberalism - the institution of the secret ballot. The trade unions oppose the use of the secret ballot by their members when voting on strike action and the like; the reason for this, say the opponents of trade unions, is that the trade union bosses want to coerce and intimidate, or at least shame, reluctant union members into going along with the majority of unionists who want a strike. The trade unionist opponents of such secret ballots argue, on the other hand, that union members should not be allowed to behave as selfish individuals, without a feeling of solidarity for their fellow workers; in voting for or against strike action, they are making decisions which affect their fellows and so should be held to account. Which is all well and good: but why do the same trade unionists oppose the use of the secret ballot in the sphere of industrial relations and at the same time endorse it at the level of state and federal politics? The system of the secret ballot at election time, where a voter thinks of himself, not as a member of a national entity, but as a furtive individual making his private choice behind a curtain in a voting booth, encourages the selfish individualism that the trade union socialist ought to want to avoid. The difference is between the public and private: the voter is voting on decisions which affect the public, i.e., the whole populace, the national well-being; but, because of the secrecy of the ballot, he is acting as a private individual. That, in the end, forces him to vote for a politician who will serve his own private, material interest.

I myself am no different from any other voter in a liberal democracy: I have voted for one mainstream, liberal democratic party or another, simply on the basis of material self-interest - I may do better, materially, under one party than the other - despite my misgivings about that party as a whole and the damage its policies could do the nation (e.g., its endorsement of a policy of unrestricted, non-white immigration). The majority of voters in a liberal democracy are in the same position: not because they are naturally selfish, anti-nationalist and have a tendency to make choices which are detrimental to the general well-being, but because they are forced to by the structure of the liberal political system.

And so the end result is that we have a multi-party system, where each party represents a certain private interest. The centre-left parties represent the trade unions (who want a government which will force employers to pay them higher wages, and give them paid maternity leave and the like); the centre-right parties represent business, small and big, who want a government which will lower the costs of doing business, by getting rid of red tape, and the obligation to pay unionized workers higher wages. And then we have parties like the Greens, whose only interest is in stopping the logging of rainforests, and enforcing global warming laws on industry (regardless of whether there is sufficient scientific evidence for global warming or not).

The nationalist thing to do would be to abolish these parties, which represent conflicting, warring interests, or amalgamate them all into one giant party which would represent the national good. And the same goes for institutions, like the trade unions and the business groups, who behave, not as members of a national community, but as economic actors motivated by their own selfish gain. (The trade unions, for instance, oppose immigration, not on nationalist grounds, but because they fear that immigrants, especially from the non-white countries, are prepared to work for less, and so will undercut the minimum wage).

And then there is that other liberal institution - the separation of powers. One of the arguments for it is that no individual, or group of individuals, can be trusted with the power of the executive, the legislature and the judiciary at the same time. Otherwise we have a system of despotism, tyranny, unrestrained by the checks and balances of the liberal parliamentary system. And liberals do not have high confidence in the discretionary power of individual statesmen: the old liberal cliché is that 'All power corrupts, and absolute power corrupts absolutely'.

I myself hold the opposite view: political office without the limitations of the separation of powers and the constitution confers a grave responsibility on the politician who holds it. By placing all the responsibility in his hands, the politician is forced to make the right decision. The economic success of the Italian Fascist and German National Socialist regimes was due to the fact that both parties had made promises - very big promises - to their electorates to restore economic life in their respective countries. The PNF and the NSDAP, and no other, were responsible for choosing the right finance ministers, the right central bank heads, in order to fulfill those promises.

Contrast that conduct with that which exists in our modern liberal democracies. Our present Australian prime minister whines that he is not responsible for high inflation and high interest rates - that is the fault of the Reserve Bank. (But he maintained before the last election in 2004 that only his government's 'good economic management' kept interest rates and inflation low). Likewise, the attitude of liberal democratic politicians in France and Germany is: 'Why should I care if unemployment and other economic and social problems are not solved in my time in office: I may be voted out at the next election anyway, and besides which, I'll always get a position on a corporate board after quitting politics, and a nice advance on my memoirs'. Again and again, there is a lack of care, a lack of responsibility, brought about, almost exclusively, by the liberal institution of the separation of powers. By diffusing power, no-one ends up holding it, and so no-one ends up bearing responsibility - for successes, or failures.

Some nations are fortunate in that, historically, there are men who have strong nationalist tendencies and who hold, at the same time, positions of power in the state. (The Weimar-era State - which, in Schmitt's view, had selfless, and nationalist-minded, men in the army, the bureaucracy and the office of Reichspräsident - is one example). These men, what Yockey calls the 'nation-bearing stratum', stand above the party politics of the day, and have a view to the national good, the good of the whole, as opposed to the good of a few economic actors. In part, this is because they are unelected: they are not, unlike the mainstream political parties, forced to cater to narrow economic and class interests.

We nationalists should aim for this 'nation-bearing' quality in government. And this, in my view, is one argument for abolishing the vote altogether. The masses, perhaps, should be allowed to signal their approval for a government through voting in plebiscites; but the practice of splitting the nation into competing, selfish individuals - through anonymous voting for parties which only represent selfish economic and class interests - should cease.

Having said that, the abolition of the separation of powers, and the practice of the secret ballot - and the ballot altogether - is not a magic bullet. None of this worked in the former Rhodesia, for example. I feel a sense of solidarity with the white Rhodesian farmers who are being oppressed, and expropriated, by the Mugabe regime, of course. But the worst thing about the Mugabe government is that it is incompetent: the economy is a mess, and is steadily eroding whatever public support Mugabe had. The whole of Africa is in such a state: even though the continent possesses some of the richest resources in the world, the politicians are too incompetent to administer them. It is hard to imagine any illiberal government in the West - Hitler's and Mussolini's, for example, or Honecker's in the former East Germany - allowing such economic disorder to continue.

VI. How to get there

Once we nationalists have swallowed any liberal qualms we may have, we are faced with the question of technique. How is the 'exception' in Western political life to occur? How are nationalists to gain constiuant pouvoir?

If we look at the history of 'white' nations in recent times which saw 'exceptions', and subsequent destructions of the liberal constitutionalist order - for instance, Chile in 1973, Greece in 1967, Argentina in 1976 - it becomes apparent that the 'exceptions' were brought about by military coup d'états. Unfortunately, the option of putschism is not available to us in the West today. The military in most Western countries is indoctrinated with the liberal dogma that military and political life are to be kept separate; furthermore, those in senior military positions who display nationalist tendencies are purged. (Again, the Allies were careful to make sure that, for example, the German army - long a bastion of German nationalism - was purged of such tendencies).

Another alternative is to follow the example of mass-based organizations like the fascist and communist movements of the 1930s, and even Arab-Muslim groups like Hezbollah and Hamas today. The method is simple: build up a following in the community, through a proliferation of community-based organizations, relentless community-activism and electioneering, until the legislature is (almost literally) encircled by the resulting mass-based, democratic movement. It was the 'struggle for the mastery of the streets' which handed the NSDAP their seats in the Reichstag state legislature; that, and their constant, disciplined, round-the-clock activist and community work (including charity work). No German town, no matter how small, was left unattended to.

Likewise, Hezbollah and Hamas function not only as political parties, but are charities, religious groups and guerrilla armies. Their lack of compromise - the sheer radicalism of their position - combined with their community work, led to the Hamas victory at the last

Palestinian elections, much to the chagrin of Israel and the West, who were hoping that the liberal Palestinians (who had no democratic mass base) would win.

It should be pointed out that the NSDAP violated another liberal tenet: parliament as a place for free and open discussion. The NSDAP and Communist Party deputies in the Reichstag were, prior to Hitler's chancellorship, notoriously rowdy and boisterous; they turned parliament into a circus - through booing, catcalling, walk-outs and other instances of disruptive behavior. Joseph Bendersky, one of Schmitt's biographers, notes, with consternation, that the NSDAP deputies received 400 points of order - that is, reprimands from the parliamentary speaker for disorderly conduct - during the Weimar period, which surely must stand as a record. The NSDAP tactics, along with their use (or perhaps one should say, abuse) of parliamentary procedure against the governments of the day, invalidated the entire parliamentary-liberal process. An application of the same methods, in Australian (or British or American) federal and state legislatures would leave the opponents of nationalism stunned; without an institutional experience of so-called 'fascist' and 'Nazi' methods, they are defenseless.

Liberals in Europe have often bewailed the fact that Italian Fascism and German National Socialism agreed to abide by the rules of liberal parliamentarism, only to destroy them when they got into power - by dissolving the separation of powers, suspending press freedom, freedom of assembly, freedom of association, the multi-party system, and the rest. The 'fascist' method, these liberals declare, was to use their parties as Trojan horses; the method is to infiltrate, and then destroy from within. (The communists, it should be pointed out, used the exact same methods (and predated the fascists in the use of these methods)). The solution is, say the liberals, to use the powers in the existing, Allied-drafted constitutions, to crush nationalism, and any instance of nationalist political 'gangsterism', from the start (likewise, any communist illiberalism must be crushed).

But, in my view, the liberal opponents of nationalism in Europe have failed to understand the strength, and the appeal, of nationalism. The NSDAP won power, not because of the Weimar constitution's article 48, but because they possessed the mass, extra-parliamentary base which conservative chancellors like Schleicher and Papen did not. So 'anti-fascist' provisions in the constitutions of Europe will do no good for the liberal cause in the long run, simply because such provisions cannot stop nationalist groups from putting roots into the community, and thereby building up a base of mass political support. (Besides which, today's nationalist groups will not repeat the same constitutional steps that the NSDAP and other fascist political parties did; constitutional history does not repeat itself, at least not exactly).

VII. The case of Whitlam

Finally, I will end with an example from recent Australian history: an example which is pertinent here, I think, because it shows how a group of politicians can fail to exploit the mass following of their party and be paralyzed by the strictures of liberal constitutionalism. I am referring to the Australian constitutional crisis of 1975, otherwise known as the Dismissal.

For non-Australian readers, or Australian readers who are unfamiliar with this episode from Australian political history, I will give a brief account. In 1975, the federal Labor government of the day was unable to pass the year's budget appropriations through the Senate, which was in control of the opposition conservatives - the Liberal and Country parties. This 'blocking of supply', i.e., blocking of the budget, was a highly unusual and unconventional parliamentary practice (but not an illegal one). At the time, however, the conservatives felt that it was warranted. They believed that they could force the Labor government to dissolve parliament and then call an election, which they felt they would win. The Labor government had been doing badly in the polls, partly because of the media agitation against it (including that by the tabloid The Sun, owned by Rupert Murdoch), and because of the outbreak of global inflation, which had plunged the Western economies into recession.

In response to the crisis, the Governor-General (the equivalent of a President in the Australian constitutional system) dismissed the Labor government, and charged the conservatives with acting as a caretaker government until parliament was dissolved and new elections were called. Despite public anger among Labor supporters and the trade union rank-and-file, the Labor Prime Minister Gough Whitlam, and the head of the Australian Council Trade Unions, Bob Hawke, accepted the dismissal because of its constitutionality. (Whitlam claimed later that, had he not accepted the dismissal, Australia would have been plunged into civil war). At the next federal election, Labor lost in a crushing landslide, and lost the two federal elections after that.

What should Whitlam have done to retain power, and ensure the passing of federal budget bill, blocked in the Senate? The answer is, he should have refused to accept the Governor-General's sacking of him; and then bussed or flown Hawke and tens of thousands of ACTU workers to Canberra, where they would have marched on Parliament House and the Governor-General's residence. Conservative senators could have been grabbed by the scruffs of their necks and then frog-marched out of the Senate, and the vote on the budget could have then taken place. The Governor-General could have been placed under house arrest. A state of emergency could have been declared, and trade unionists working for, for instance, The Sun newspaper, could have gone on strike. The Labor government could then have proceeded to pass law after law, and make amendments to the constitution (without going through the usual route of having national referenda on those amendments). Opposition parties could have been outlawed, and riot police, soldiers and trade union thugs used to break up opposition meetings and rallies. Newspaper proprietors, like Murdoch, could have been forced to toe the line or face compulsory expropriation without compensation. Elections, in the meanwhile, could have been suspended - indefinitely.

All of this would have been blatantly illegal, but within the bounds of political possibility. After all, the trade union movement in Australia in the 1970s was massive - Australia being one of the most unionized countries in the Western world - and powerful; it would have been quite capable of bringing the country to a standstill. They had the power, they had the numbers, they had the force - and, in the days of 1975, the militancy.

While the Australian economy was deteriorating, and a good many Australians doubtless wanted to see Whitlam voted out, the fact is that the Labor Party at the point possessed a significant mass-base in the trade union movement (and in the left-wing intellectuals, and public sector workers), ready to be deployed for extra-parliamentary action. But they were not mobilized. Why? Because, in the end, Whitlam and Hawke were liberal constitutionalists, liberal (meaning prepared to abide by the existing constitutional order) socialists. They were not prepared to cross the line of legality and constitutionality as, for instance, both Allende and Pinochet had done a few years before in Chile.

Perhaps, too, it was a question of timing: a revolution against parliamentary democracy should have been carried out at the start of Whitlam's rule - when Labor had won federal elections in 1972. The right amount of constitutional violations, and suppression of the conservative opposition, would have spared his government problems further on down the line.

Whitlam failed, in the end, because he was a liberal democrat. We nationalists, if we are not to make the same mistakes, must be democrats - but not liberal.

8

WE ARE THE LEFT? THE RIGHT? WHATEVER!!!!!!!!!

1. Introduction

This is an article which explores questions of tactics and propaganda, building on previous articles such as "On Kameradschaft" and "The Power of the People." Most of its suggestions - regarding demos, leaflets, posters, etc. - are not easily put into practice straight away. Simply put, at the present stage we do not have the numbers, in Australia, at least, to carry out large demonstrations, and we do not possess all the requisite materials and equipment for making posters, and the rest, on the scale that the Left in this country does (and what is more, of the same quality). Having said that, I think it is important that we nationalists, at this early stage, start considering these things. This article, like previous ones in this vein, will be drawing upon the example of certain German nationalist movements - the Freie Kameradschaften, the Freie Nationalisten, and the Autonome Nationalisten - as well as the NPD itself.

It should be noted that throughout the essay, I will be using the terms 'left' and 'right' in their conventional sense. This is not to say that I do not recognize their limitations. (For instance, most nationalists are characterized by mainstream analysts as 'Far Right', which is, I think, woefully inaccurate). What is more, I consider a good many political issues (especially ones relevant to nationalism) to be 'beyond left and right'.

Unlike many, I tend to characterize the German nationalism of the NPD and the Freie Nationalisten groups as 'left-wing' and 'socialist'. I also think that, to a great extent, the nationalist movement is left-wing and socialist. What I am advocating here is that we place those 'socialist', anti-globalist and anti-capitalist elements to the forefront of our doctrine, and that we repackage certain parts of our image (as it is conveyed in our visual propaganda (posters, symbols, leaflets, banners, etc.) and our slogans to get that across. By doing that, we will appeal to a wider cross-section of the politically thinking, conscious community which is left-leaning, anti-globalist and anti-capitalist. We will then manage to compete, successfully, with the mainstream Left (the anarchists, communists, social democrats and liberals, plus the trade unionists and environmentalists). The mainstream Left was able to claim a monopoly on political issues like anti-globalization and the environment. That is, anyone who was concerned with these things was naturally on the (mainstream) Left. Nationalism has to work to break that monopoly.

As well as that, the Left seems to have a monopoly on the young - it is easier to attract a young person into the folds of the Left than it is into the nationalist 'Far Right'. The reason for that is that the Left are politically active, forming groups and holding demonstrations; but they also portray themselves, in their propaganda, as rebels and underdogs - something which is appealing to the young. But the 'underdog' and 'rebel' status can easily be appropriated for nationalism, and for the most part, it is a question of adopting the Left's symbolism and imagery (which I will discuss later).

2. What is Left and what is socialist?

On one level, socialism is about redistributing wealth. Under the market system, some people are rich, and others are poor, most are in between. The socialist view is that certain distributions of wealth are unjust - that is, certain groups deserve more than they are allocated by the market system - and so the government, and collective action, has to step in and redistribute it. Hugo Chavez is a typical socialist. His followers, the slum dwellers of Caracas and other parts of Venezuela, deserve more, in Chavez' view, than they have received under previous neo-liberal governments. His intention, then, is to redistribute wealth. He does this by, among other things, nationalizing American-owned oil refineries: the profits are to no longer go to Yanqui, gringo shareholders, but to 'the people' - Venezuelans, or at least, the neediest, who happen to be Chavez' followers. Nationalization and welfarism are the two main tools of 'government' socialism.

Other socialisms, however, need not be as extreme, polarizing and confrontational as Chavez'. Indeed, socialism can exist within a mainstream liberal democratic context. Mainstream social democrat or liberal-socialist parties can and do use the tools of nationalization and welfarism (more the latter than the former) to redistribute wealth. Even the conservative-leaning National Party in Australia is an agrarian socialist party, redistributing taxpayer's money to 'rural and regional Australia'. (One of the great ironies of Australian politics is that the Nationals are in a coalition with the free-market conservative Liberal Party). Indigenous groups in Australia, and Afro-American groups in America, likewise seek a share of taxpayer's money - in the name of 'social justice', redressing inequality and compensating for past injustices (e.g., slavery, or the theft, by white settlers, of indigenous land).

There are, of course, the Marxist socialisms. Socialism in Marx's time, and for many decades afterwards, had its roots in the working classes, who were exploited by capitalism. Like Dickens, Marx viewed Victorian capitalism as gloomy, degrading, soul-destroying; Marx was outraged over practices like child labor, for instance. The solution proffered by the communists, and other advocates of working-class socialism, was nationalization, welfare and legislation against exploitative practices.

Over time, 'working-class socialism' filtered through to mainstream liberal socialist parties, like the German SPD and the British Labor Party, but not necessarily through Marx (Britain, for instance, has a strong, non-Marxist Fabian socialist tradition).

After the war, 'national' communisms sprang up in the Third World; but, for Cuban, Vietnamese and Chinese communism, the peasantry, and not the blue-collar proletariat of the cities, were the agents of revolutionary change. Marx's theory, by this point, had been twisted beyond recognition, but the Third World communists still insisted on categorizing themselves as Marxist.

What of nationalism - Western nationalism? It has been argued elsewhere on this site that the German National Socialist and Italian Fascist movements and their imitators were socialist and left-wing in their orientation. Their membership included many disgruntled ex-communists and sympathizers or members from the mainstream liberal democratic socialist parties. Likewise, the NPD's ideology has a socialist tone. Its party program implies that the existing neo-liberal order is unfair to the indigenous Germans, and that wealth should be redistributed - not to Kurdish or Turkish immigrants, but to indigenous German families, particularly in the depressed areas of the East.

But there are additional reasons to characterize nationalism as socialist. For one thing, nationalists are naturally against globalization, specifically the globalization of people. In the neo-liberal and capitalist order, all human beings are interchangeable labor units, without any defining ethnic, racial or cultural characteristics. Or, if they have those characteristics, they hardly matter. So, if a few hundred thousand immigrants arrive from a Third World country to France, Germany, Australia or America, it will make no difference to the economy. Indeed, immigrants are 'good for' the economy, because, among other things, immigrants are quite generously prepared to work hard enough to pay for not only their social security pensions but the rest of the population's as well. For these reasons, according to business, we should ignore any effect immigration, and the corresponding changes in demographics, have on the existing culture. Big business is globalist, and supports immigration in order to obtain cheap labor. But ironically, the Left supports this side of globalization, and welcomes immigration as well (albeit for different reasons).

Sectors of the community other than business are prepared to welcome immigration for quite selfish and stupid reasons. Recently, the CFMEU (the Construction, Forestry, Mining and Engineering Union, one of Australia's largest) has undertaken a campaign to have immigrant workers naturalized - in the hope that they will vote against the incumbent anti-union Liberal Party. Such a mentality betrays a selfish, short-term outlook - an outlook which is more associated, in leftist polemics, with capitalism than anything else: that view is 'Only my economic interests matter, no-one else's'. We nationalists reject that, considering that to be destructive to the community and the common good.

Then there are the economists, who are always cobbling together good sound 'economic' reasons for immigration. They claim that the ageing population in the West will place a strain on our social security systems, so we will need immigrants to pay for tax money for those pensions, but to replenish our numbers. As well as that, economists think that the addition of consumers (most economists today think in terms of demand-side economics, which places the consumer at the center) will likewise be 'good for the economy'.

But all these are rationalizations. There are plenty of other good economic reasons for rejecting immigration: for one, Australia does not have an unlimited supply of natural resources (like water); some studies show immigration to be bad for the environment; and so on.

The main reason why nationalists reject immigration is that we place a high value on the homogenous, and harmonious, community. And it is this concern with community and solidarity which we share with the mainstream Left. In 'An Infantile Disorder? Crisis and Decline of the New Left' (1977), Nigel Young writes (of the New Left in America):

The 'myth' of community was a central one for the [New Left] movement; Georges Sorel had once used the notion of myth to depict something that was not necessarily untrue or impossible, but an image of the future which guided effective action in the present; a truth becoming rather than existing. Such was the idea of community in the growth of the NL and the counter-culture, reflecting the influence of anarchist and utopian socialist ideas, and filtered through writers like Fromm and Goodman; but it also reflected a general popular and sociological concern with a 'loss of community'; in the words of the Port Huron Statement itself, the task was 'bringing people out of isolation and into community'.

That was a function of politics. For Mills, 'mass society' described an atomized, amorphous social situation in which individuation had replaced true individualism: conformity replaced autonomy, leaving only the alienation of 'pseudo-gemeinschaft', a phony community of status-striving, the success ethic and the rat-race. This society elevated individualism as an ideal, but undermined its social basis. Both the cult of organizational belongingness and the quite contradictory myth of competitive individualism are cultivated to disguise the real nature of the corporate conveyor belt. (p. 57).

These are some of the key tenets of Leftism and Socialism: the isolating, alienating effects of capitalism and liberal individualism; and the need to increase community bonds, a sense of fellow-feeling and shared destiny, and have members of the community work, at least in part, for the good of the whole instead of their own selfish benefit. That can be accomplished through a number of ways: Lenin, Adolf Hitler, Mao Tse Tung, Castro, Gamel Nasser, Huey Long, Juan Peron, each had their different answers to the question. And these are only the 'government' socialisms: there are the 'libertarian' socialisms as well - the anarchists and the counter-culture dropouts who formed their own communes.

It is reasonable to say that many of the ideologists of early socialism and anarchism would certainly be "racist" by today's standards. Marx and Engels intended communism for industrial societies in the First World like England and Germany. Had they, and other socialists of Germany in the 19th century, been told that future communists would support mass immigration into the West with a view to making Germans a minority, they would have been appalled, not to mention astounded.

3. The New Left and its relevance to nationalism

In view of this, it is worth recounting the history of the New Left, which has lessons for nationalists. The New Left was a mass, left-wing radical movement in the West which began in the 1950s but gained prominence in the 1960s, and died sometime in the 1970s. The New Left championed women's rights, desegregation, environmentalism, gay rights, mass non-white immigration, nuclear disarmament, and campaigned for an end to the war in Vietnam. It looked to communists like Che, Mao, and Ho Chi Minh as heroes, but represented a break from the 'old' Left (Leninism, Stalinism, Trotskyism). Unlike the 'old' Left, it had its membership base, not in the working-class trade union movement, or in Leninist 'revolutionary vanguards' (small groups of communist activists, often working undercover and infiltrating mainstream political groups), but in students and youth (mostly white and middle class). Culturally, its roots were deep within the sixties Hippie counter-culture of the time.

The movement burned out for a number of reasons: its use of violence, culminating, among the more radical groups (like the Weathermen and the Red Army Faction), in a campaign of urban guerrilla warfare against the State; infiltration by the 'old' Left groups who steered the movement in a more pro-Moscow, pro-Beijing direction; psychological strains imposed by drugs, communal living, sexual promiscuity and other elements of drop-out counter-culture life; organizational problems; and changing political and economic circumstances.

Perhaps most important of all, they failed to win over the support of the working classes and other significant groups in the community. Partially this was because of the natural conservatism and apathy in sections of the Western working classes of that time, and the generation gap between the old, working-class, trade union types and the young radicals. But it was also due to the fact that, as the seventies progressed, the behavior of the New Left alienated people who could have been the

New Left's natural supporters.

While nationalists may find large parts of their program noxious, there is much we can learn from it. On a close examination, it becomes clear that New Leftism has much in common with National Anarchism and the Freie Nationalisten/Freie Kameradschaften/ Autonome Nationalisten movements. The New Left doctrine emphasized spontaneous 'organization without disorganization'; activism over theory; activism directed towards the concerns of today rather than tomorrow; extra-parliamentarism; a non-hierarchical, amorphous structure (meaning that there were no strict membership rules and no leadership which imposes orders and rules from the top down); the creation of a parallel society and 'counter-institutions' (i.e. community activist groups which to a certain extent usurp the functions of the State - 'We visualize and then build structures to counter those which we oppose', in the words of Tom Hayden). All in all, it preferred to be a 'movement' over a 'party'. The New Left groups were decentralized and difficult for an outside agency (like the government) to infiltrate and control.

All of this had its basis on anarchist theory. As Young writes:

The NL's version of pluralism sought the representation of all social groups regardless of their power or literacy or degree of organization... Mills's 'publics', Goodman's and Fromm's 'community', Lynd's and Hayden's 'participatory democracy', all point towards a recreation of a genuine and 'socialist' pluralism. Such concepts also provide a base for a more utopian and anarchistic sociology; populist, eclectic and experimental, 'from the bottom-upwards' - in tune with decentralized movement projects, and making possible, in contrast, a sociology of the structures of unfreedom, of war, the State, and revolutionary limitation and possibility.

Thus these libertarian radicals of the 1960s largely accepted an end to doctrinaire solutions and closed utopias, endorsing the sort of pluralism and flexibility that had been characteristic of much anarchist thought.

The projection of a single historical sequence, the single blueprint for a new society, the unified and reductionist theory of man or history, [all the elements of Marxist theory], was replaced by an insistence on the need for different groups, a range of solutions. (Young, pp. 22-23).

Part of this came about from a disillusionment with party politics and elections. Left-wing activists had placed great faith in mainstream liberal or social democratic politicians, only to be burned each time. (The nationalist in Australia who reads of this cannot help but be reminded of the Pauline Hanson-One Nation experience). As well as that, the Old Left tactic of infiltrating mainstream center-left parties and institutions, and gradually turning them towards a communist party line, was not working; neither were the communist parties which competed in elections (an option available to them after the McCarthyite anti-communist phase of American political life had ceased).

More than that, however, was a desire, on the part of the many impetuous young activists who made up the New Left, to do something now. In an ideal left-wing world, a communist party would come to power through the ballot box and start expropriating the capitalist class and redistributing wealth. But clearly that was not possible in Europe and America in the 1960s, at least in the short term. Which raised the question: given that the Left lacked the political power to do what it wanted, how could it go about building a socialist community today? How could one bring about an order where one can feel a sense of solidarity, kinship and community, and work for the well-being of the whole (instead of the individual)? How could one escape the confines of the liberal capitalist order straight away?

The simple truth was that the institutions of communism were designed to benefit the people - not the other way around. Forced collectivizations, expropriation without compensation, rationing, price controls, currency controls, a hierarchical state management of state-owned enterprises, the abolition of profit, interest, competition - all the techniques of communism - were intended to increase man's well-being. Obviously, this was not apparent from the way the communist regimes of China, Russia, Cuba and Vietnam worked: to the anti-Marxist New Leftist, these regimes were 'anti-people'. Communism had lost sight of the truths of socialism, and persisted in treating people like objects - a carry-over from capitalism. Under a business-friendly liberal democratic regime, business manipulates the government in order to serve business; while under communism, the government manipulates the people in order to serve the government.

So New Leftism sought to create socialism on the ground. 'The underground society grows out of the ground now, and it begins - independent of the still ruling authorities - to live its life and to rule itself' (Young, p.93).

All of this is relevant to nationalism for a number of reasons. Populists and nationalists tend to wait for the big electoral breakthrough, for the messiah who, at the head of a party, will take control of the government, in a Leninist-style, Bolshevik revolution (or Hitler-style, National Socialist revolution) and do all the things that they have wanted: expel immigrants; cut ties to Israel; begin expropriating the assets (particularly media and entertainment assets) of capitalists who are antipathetic to nationalism. But all these policies are intended to bring about a sense of unification and solidarity among peoples of European descent in the West. They aim to replace the old, deracinated, neo-liberal consumer order with one which could be described as 'socialist', or at least communitarian. Given that we cannot achieve this, at present, through the ballot box, how can we work towards it now?

Part of the answer, I feel, lies in the formation of small, decentralized groups of 'autonomous nationalists', as detailed in 'The Power of the People'. Capitalist, consumerist society is isolating and alienating (even without large numbers of non-white immigrants); we can break that down, in the nationalist community, by encouraging nationalists to associate with one another, in a 'disorganized' manner, without coercion. That is the first step. One of the benefits of that approach is that it makes the individual nationalist realize that he is not alone - and that he can draw strength, in an individualist, anti-racial world, from being in a group.

This has relevance, too, for non-white groups. Recently, the conservative Australian government has unveiled a raft of policies designed to assist isolated, squalid indigenous communities, which, like indigenous communities in North America, suffer from alcoholism, drug abuse, poverty, and low life expectancy. In these communities, which are tantamount to reservations, social pathologies, like child abuse, and spousal abuse, are rampant. Over the past few decades, a large industry of welfare and social workers has sprung up to tend to the needs of the indigenous, but cannot have said to have helped them much at all. So the government is looking for other solutions, and is, with its latest policies, for the most part winning the applause of conservatives in the press, and the qualified support of the opposition Labor Party.

But in the 'debate' on how to 'save' the indigenous people of Australia from themselves, no-one has looked at the possible solution of mutual aid. That is, the indigenous people in these communities could form activist groups and concentrate on improving their lives, without control and direction from the government and the indigenous welfare agencies. They could do simple things like clean up graffiti, carry out renovations of run-down government-owned properties, and prevent the supply of liquor.

The conservatives like to preach the value of 'self-help'; their belief is that indigenous people should lift themselves up by the bootstraps and leave their fellows behind. But a far better approach, in my view, is mutual aid - people co-operating in groups to benefit their community. And what can work for the indigenous people can work for the whites.

4. The revolutionary agency

In Marxist theory of the 'imminent' communist revolution and the downfall of capitalism, the working-class plays the central part - or rather, the working-class organized into a mass communist party. After receiving a proper political education in the truths of Marxism and dialectical materialism, the proletarian will see the truth of 'scientific socialism', develop class consciousness, and feel a radical antipathy towards capitalism. The revolution comes about through a violent overthrow of capitalism, the bourgeoisie, and liberal democracy; or it comes about when the masses come to see the good sense of communist practice and then simply vote the pro-capitalist political parties out.

This side of Marxism presented a problem for the New Left. For one, the working classes in the West in the 1960s were not revolutionary, but, through the massive trade union movement (e.g., the AFL-CIO) were very much part of the liberal democratic order. As well as that, the trade unionists were racist, nationalist and very much opposed to desegregation and civil rights for Negroes. They were antipathetic to the pro-Hanoi, anti-colonialist foreign policy orientation of the New Left as well.

It was this lack of revolutionary potential in the working classes that led the theorists of the New Left to scout around for a new 'revolutionary agency'. Accordingly, the New Left made a fetish of Negroes struggling for civil rights, or the 'peasants' of Indochina waging an anti-colonialist war against the Americans and their puppets; some New Leftists even made a cult of the lumpenproletarian, following a strand in early anarchist thought.

These social or racial groups were said to have the dynamic potential which would bring about the revolution against capitalism. But, in the end, the New Leftists had to face up to the obvious: most of their membership was (mostly) white middle-class students. Speaking of C. Wright Mills, one of the leading New Left intellectuals, Young writes:

Mills... having written off the disorganized poor, the co-opted blacks and working-class leadership, the accommodated unions and the middle class dominated by consumerism and bureaucratism, continued his search for the 'insurgent impulse' where it could be found... [It] led usually back to the radical young and the activist students. By the early 1960s, they had already taken a leading part in European peace movements; students also played a continuing role in internal change (such as the overthrow of Menderes in Turkey, and Synghman Rhee in Korea) and after 1960, their role in Japan and Latin America became a constant echo of actions taken in North America and Europe. (Young, p. 110).

At once, the critic can see that a movement which has its base located in students and youth would experience severe problems. They could not be said to exist as a unified group, a class, or have much in the way of political clout. As Young writes:

How could seven million students, mostly white, mostly middle class, ever be a class in themselves? Student culture, despite the enormous impact of the New Left as a movement, was by no means solidary. External ties, training differentiation, seniority, size of student community, living situations, and finally sex and race, were all factors that could cut across the solidarity of students. As in the development of all classes, occupational and interest differentiation will be the most stubborn obstacle to the development of communal identity. Engineers versus humanities students, those whose first priority is exam-taking against those whose objective is the humanization of the university environment, is paralleled by the opposition between craft and industrial unionism, between different racial groups, between the individual striver and the collective solidarist, which has characterized the history of classes in modern societies...

On behalf of the concept of a student class, it could be argued that this student interlude was at least a time of maximum volatility when the purchase of society was less strong. But for all this, the likelihood that students could organize effectively on a national scale as a political force, was small...

Perhaps the most telling opposition to the use of the class label for the student community came from those who stressed the evanescent quality of the status. Even if a majority of twenty million high-school leavers in the USA went through university, it remained an interim time for most of them; rarely lasting more than four years, the stakes in it are not that high. (Young, p.111).

Despite such dire prognostications, the student movement was spectacularly successful - gaining numbers, in America, at least, that American nationalists can at present only dream about:

By 1968, student support in America may have stood at around a million sympathizers, of whom probably 150,000 were actively linked to the movement or its organizations (e.g. by membership), over half of these were linked to SDS [Students for a Democratic Society], locally or nationally. Certainly, by 1968 and 1969, SDS itself was undeniably numerically larger than ever, and with 60,000-100,000 members of local chapters, by far the largest organization on the Left...

A movement which had begun with a few thousands on a few major campuses (the large and prestigious, usually state, universities) had, after the Columbia rebellion, spread to literally every campus in America down to the smallest junior college; and even in black colleges in the South, where a new wave of militancy was apparent in1968, comparable movements existed. (Young, p.188).

5. We need students and youth

I will now advance a thesis that most nationalists will find controversial: in order for a nationalist revolution to succeed, we must target the students. It is an axiom of modern political life that no revolution has ever succeeded without the support of the students - whether it be in Weimar Germany or Batista's Cuba. It is almost certain that, once the universities go, the rest of a country's institutions go. Which is why reactionaries, like the Pinochet Junta in Chile, made it a point to target the universities first: in order to get rid of communism, and nip any revolution in the bud, they had to invade the universities and purge them of left-wing students, who, in Allende's Chile, were quite numerous.

In contemporary times, the communist groups in Australia manage to recruit among the students with great success. At the least, the memberships of the two main groups - Socialist Alliance and Socialist Alternative - respectively run into the hundreds. After the communist student members graduate, they go on take jobs in the public service (of course) and plough money back into their parties. The same phenomenon occurred in the New Left: the post-graduates employed in the capitalist system would even form groups with names like 'Radicals in the Professions'.

Nationalists, I know, will object to targeting students because a good many nationalists, or potential supporters of nationalism in the community, are not middle-class and not university-educated. For one, they may be afraid of the better education of students, or at least, afraid of the unknown quantity that these people represent.

To this I respond that we do not want to reject people who do not fit in the student or ex-student category: merely that we want to pitch our propaganda, our approach, to the levels of the student. Hollywood marketers today aim their blockbuster films at audiences with a mental age of 13 (which is one of the reasons why so many Hollywood films are awful). People who are older than 13, or are smarter than a 13 year old, will still go and see a piece of rubbish like Shrek 4 or whatever; but the target audience is someone with the intelligence of the 13 year old. Likewise, we nationalists should be trying to appeal with someone with the tastes and intelligence of the modern college student. Certainly, we do not want to attract people only from the student class: we want to (unlike the New Left) attract the parents of these students - the white middle-classes (see a previous essay at New Right Australia, "The Radicalization of the Middle Classes"). But we need a base which is already, to an extent, radicalized; has a lot of time on its hands for activism (and most people in the professions are simply too busy); and is aware of, and concerned with, the problems of the world. Students and youth fit the bill perfectly.

We should not underestimate the radical potential of the student body. It surprised and upset quite a few Marxist theorists when (especially during the uprising in France in May 1968) it was shown that it was the middle-class student who was the radical socialist, and not the proletarian. But the (non-Marxist), New Left anarchist Murray Bookchin understood. Speaking of the 'non-revolutionary' characteristics of the working class, he wrote:

The worker becomes a revolutionary not by becoming more of a worker but by undoing his "workerness"... His "workerness" is the disease he is suffering from, the social affliction telescoped to individual dimensions... The worker begins to become a revolutionary when he undoes his "workerness", when he comes to detest his class status here and now, when he begins to disgorge exactly those features which the Marxists most prize in him: his work ethic, his characterology derived from industrial discipline, his respect for hierarchy, his obedience to leaders, his consumerism, his vestiges of puritanism. In this sense, the worker becomes a revolutionary to the degree that he sheds his class status and achieves an un-class consciousness. He degenerates - and he degenerates magnificently. What he is shedding are precisely those class shackles that bind him to all systems of domination. He abandons those class interests that enslave him to consumerism, suburbia and a bookkeeping conception of life... (Bookchin, 'Listen, Marxist!' in "All we are saying..." : the philosophy of the New Left, ed. Arthur Lothstein, p.105).

What happens is a process of hippie-fication or bohemianisation:

The most promising development in the factories today is the emergence of young workers who smoke pot, f*ck-off on their jobs, drift into and out of factories, grow long or longish hair, demand more leisure time than more pay, steal, harass all authority figures, go on wildcats, and turn on their fellow workers. Even more promising is the emergence of this human type in trade schools and high schools, the reservoir of the industrial working class to come. To the degree that workers, vocational students, and high school students link their life-styles to various aspects of the anarchic youth culture, to that degree will the proletariat be transformed from a force for the conservation of the established order into a force for revolution. (Bookchin, p.105).

The fact of the matter is that the blue-collar working classes are a conservative bunch, and working-class culture is, at its worse, coarse and brutal. A hundred years ago, working-class people in Britain attended night classes to receive an education in arts, culture, and the humanities, or read popularizations of science and philosophy in order to 'better' themselves. In other words, they were striving to achieve (what they perceived to be) the refinement and sophistication of the middle-classes, who had the leisure and the income to cultivate themselves. Now, however, in Britain, the working-class ethic reigns supreme, in the media, popular culture, but, apparently, in the social life of Britons itself: even people of 'good', respectable middle-class backgrounds affect coarse, crude mannerisms and working-class accents in order to fit in and appear 'working class'. (The reason is that the middle classes, over the past few decades, have been demonized in British popular culture, television, and film; whereas, the working-

137

classes are portrayed as having warmth, humanity, and integrity. Needless to say, the average British scriptwriters tend to be members of the politically correct master race in terms of their political sympathies).

So a certain amount of education and cultivation, no matter how small, is essential to make someone less self-centered, more cognizant of the problems of the world - aware of what globalization is, for example, or what Zionism is, or the fact that there are wars in Iraq and Afghanistan going on right now (and the reasons why these wars are taking place). This is necessary for an individual to reach his or her revolutionary potential. And this is the point that Bookchin is trying to make. (The same process of education occurs in nationalism. The average nationalist, in my view, often possesses more knowledge of political theory and history, and the history of the European peoples, than the average person - certainly more than the average blue-collar worker). Even the proletarian who goes on to become an active socialist in a social democratic party must, to a certain extent, educate himself, refine himself and overcome his 'workerness'.

In the student class, fortunately, we have ready-made radicals: people who are more than ready to 'smash the system'.

I am not suggesting that nationalists campaign on campuses on student issues - e.g., more funding for better student services and the like (although if activists want to do that, they should go ahead). What I am suggesting is that we nationalists do not put, in our propaganda, anything which will make the average student run a mile. It should be a general rule of thumb that, if a piece of propaganda scares students, white, middle-class, and left-leaning youth, and fails to appeal to them, then it won't appeal to anyone.

As a concrete example, take Tom Metzger's White Aryan Resistance website, with its online racist computer games (where one has to shoot as many illegal Mexican immigrants as one can before they cross the border, and so on). I am not being puritanical and politically-correct about such games - I personally find them amusing, as do quite a few other nationalists. But the average non-nationalist student, for instance, finds them shocking and horrifying, and will have his worst impressions of nationalism confirmed by them. For that reason, most of what is on Metzger's site should be rejected, and certainly we can find things more important and relevant to the nationalist cause than silly online racist computer games, or racist cartoons.

6. Symbols and slogans

The other thing we have to do is become more and more left-wing in our appearance. To achieve this, we merely have to change the form, not the content. The German nationalist groups, especially the Freie Nationalisten, in my opinion show us the way. They use Che, Hugo Chavez, Castro; quote left-wing notables like Friedrich Engels and Ernst Thälmann (the former German communist party leader); wear the standard anarchist 'uniform' (sunglasses, black baseball cap, black hoodie, and even black scarves wrapped around their faces) at demonstrations; and they demonstrate against globalization (at G-20 meetings, for instance) or against Zionism (some even wear Arab headscarves to show their solidarity with the Palestinians). In their posters, slogans, badges, banners, and their look, they replicate the feel of the Left, particularly the anti-globalization 'black bloc' Left.

The approach has a number of advantages. Firstly, their look (and politics is as much about the visual as it is about theory) fits in with the 'student' Left', the bohemian 'youth', and so has that edge of hipness about it. Secondly, the posters, fliers, badges, etc., are radical and socialist enough, but innocuous enough to be displayed anywhere - at a campus, on a street corner, even in an office (I know this from experience): when people see them, their first reaction, after digesting the message, is to consider it to be standard left-wing propaganda - not "Nazi" or "racist" at all. Third, the Antifa at demonstrations against nationalism wear the anarchist 'uniform' as well - dressing like them acts as camouflage and confuses not only them but the police. Fourth, using "left"-type visual propaganda annoys the (conventional Marxist and anarchist) Left intensely, which is its own reward. (One anti-nationalist writer on the Internet even accuses the Freie Nationalisten of trying to appropriate the power of the Left as if all the badges, slogans, clothing, etc., of the Left were the sources of shamanic, mystical power. The Freie Nationalisten often use a two-flag symbol which has the reverse colors of the German Antifa; the militant Anti-Antifa uses for its symbol a parody of the Antifa 'Good night white pride' symbol and logo - 'Good night Left side'). The fifth advantage is that it breaks down conventional Left-Right thinking among non-nationalists, who previously thought that boycotting McDonald's and Starbucks was a 'Left' concern.

The most important thing is image. One only has to compare an anti-Semitic cartoon image produced by the likes of Tom Metzger's White Aryan Resistance (which has specialized in cartoons of that kind for a while) with a "left"-looking anti-Zionist, pro-Palestinian poster. The nationalist who is anti-Zionist could either come up with a poster depicting a Jew as a rat, or pointing out how many Jews are involved in the American pornography industry, or how many media assets are owned by Jews, etc.; or he could use a photo of a Palestinian boy throwing stones at an Israeli tank, and place, across the top, a slogan like 'Defy Israel!'. The latter is not "Nazi", not "racially offensive" and can be plastered on walls of buildings in the city centre, or on campus, without attracting media attention.

And what of all the symbols associated with nationalism: Celtic crosses, '14/88' symbols, swastikas, variants on the NSDAP flag, SS symbols, Thor hammers, and Nordic-looking runes? These stick out like a sore thumb, and brand one as "Nazi" or "white supremacist" straight away. Far better to subvert an existing left-wing symbol: for instance, a common Frei Nationalist badge has the Antifa 'two flags' symbol with the slogan 'Nationale Sozialisten - Bundesweite Aktion' logo or the slogan 'Frei, Sozial and National' against a plain black "anarchist" backdrop. A black t-shirt will have, in German, the slogan 'No war for Israel! Against Zionism!' with the 'two flags' symbol. A banner will read, 'Against globalization and capitalism' - a slogan not out of keeping with German National Socialism or Italian Fascism, but one which is contemporary Left as well.

Anarchist symbols often show men in masks and beanies, or men (or boys) using slingshots, or men about to throw molotov cocktails. The symbols have a message; they signify a number of things - defiance; radicalism; a war waged by the little people using the weapons of the weak. They are anti-authoritarian, and have the benefit of evoking the underdog, which is a big psychological advantage in propaganda. They are also radical and edgy enough to attract the youth, students and those who want to look different from the crowd (and who, paradoxically, want to fit in with their student or bohemian peer group). As well as that, anarchist visual propaganda uses images of masked people - which symbolises that anarchism is anonymous, that anyone can be an anarchist.

In contrast, the Metzger cartoons, for instance, represent ugliness and hate (which, again, is not to say that they cannot be amusing). And the white pride/Neo-Nazi symbols have disadvantages which are obvious.

Having said this, it is a matter of externals. If a nationalist wants to wear white pride, etc., tattoos on his body, or festoon swastikas and other symbols around his home, he should feel free to do so. But, at rallies, and in designing propaganda posters, websites and the like, it is more advantageous to adopt the Left look (especially the clothing, which preserves one's anonymity - sunglasses, hoods and caps do obscure one's features remarkably in photos).

Ironically, much of modern nationalism uses imagery and symbols which are at least seventy to eighty years out of date. The original fascist movements of the 1920s and 1930s stood on the cutting edge when they first appeared - politically, intellectually, culturally. They were avant-garde (which was one of the reasons why they appealed to so many of Europe's intellectuals, and artists). But today's nationalist movements look back to the past - using old National Socialist symbols, posters, flags, and even uniforms (if one is a Nutzi). (Italian and British Fascist imagery is recycled too, to a certain extent). Australian nationalists use Eureka Stockade flags, and make a cult of old Australian national icons, like Ned Kelly and Henry Lawson - who were antiquated even before the onset of the fascist and Bolshevist era. Nationalists, it seems, cannot help living in the past.

Readers of Hitler's 'Mein Kampf' will recall Hitler's impressions of the first time he experienced Marxist visual propaganda in a German city - great red banners, parades, rallies, and the like - and the feelings of awe it gave him. He quickly realized that he had to appropriate the visual style of the Left, because that was a big part of the Left's appeal. For the same reasons, Mussolini's Fascists copied the Left's style. Supposing that these two men were alive today, and sought to imitate the Left - how would they go about it? Certainly, leftism has changed since the 1920s. The face of today's leftism is not the hammer and sickle, and the proletarian working-man in overalls and a cap, but the black outfits of the anarchist radicals at the 1999 WTO conference in Seattle (the 'Battle of Seattle') or the demonstrations against the G-20 summit Rostock, Germany in 2007. The icons of left-wing iconography are not Marx, Engels, Trotsky, Lenin and Stalin, but Hugo Chavez, Subcomandante Marcos of the Mexican Chiapas movement, and Che, whose appeal continues to endure. The Left has moved on; it has even moved on from the days of the New Left in the sixties (whose icons were Ho Chi Minh, Mao, and the Black Panthers).

But it is not merely a matter of a nationalist "Far Right" appropriating the outer trappings of leftism. One of the slogans of the student uprising in May, 1968 was, 'The consumer society must perish a violent death. The society of alienation must disappear from history. We are inventing a new and original world'. That is what we nationalists are trying to achieve: an overcoming of the alienation the members of the white race, the peoples of the West, feel towards one another, brought about by the neo-liberal ideology, which substitutes the satisfactions of consumerism for racial and national belonging.

Having said this, there are quite a few genuinely right-wing people in the nationalist movement. The American nationalist movement has plenty of small-government; classical liberal types who would ordinarily vote Republican; likewise, many of the Far Right populist parties in Europe are that - Far Right, ultraconservative and reactionary.

This, in my view, has to be discarded. We nationalists have to change - by becoming more youthful and forward-looking. The British National Party campaigns heavily in parts of Britain which are disadvantaged; they pitch their appeal at white Britons who feel, not unjustly, that non-white immigrants get better government services than they do, simply because of the reverse racism of a succession of PC governments which values immigrants more than indigenous Britons. One of the BNP's slogans is, 'We're the Labor Party your granddad used to vote for'. I sympathize with that sentiment; had I been a Briton in 1960, or even in 1970, I would have voted Labor. But I would much prefer it if the BNP changed their slogan to, 'We're the radicals who rioted at Seattle in 1999'.

7. Objections

If I have persuaded 50 or more nationalists to follow the Freie Nationalist lead, and put together a demonstration at an anti-globalization (or anti-Iraq war, or anti-Israel) march, and dress as "anarchists", and carry "left-seeming" banners, and cover up any Nordic rune tattoos - then I have accomplished my purpose here.

But there are potential pitfalls, which I will now point out. Part of the downfall of the New Left was its embrace of violence. It preached the doctrine of 'direct action', which at first translated into civil disobedience, peaceful protest and draft-dodging and then became a rationale for rioting, the 'occupation' of university classrooms, 'trashing' of rooms and the like, before winding up in guerrilla violence - bombings, kidnappings, hijackings, and assassinations. Likewise, the anti-globalization movement has a reputation for mindless violence.

The violence at the 1999 WTO conference, and the publicity given to it, was unprecedented. In my experience, many people who observed it on the television felt at the time that the anti-globalization demonstrators did have a genuine grievance (which justified to a certain extent the violence and destruction of property). But, by the time of the 2006 G-20 summit in Melbourne last year - which included assaults on police and police vehicles by protestors - the general public, in my view, had become somewhat impatient with the violent anti-globalization crowd, characterizing it as nihilistic violence and destruction of property for its own sake. The average violent anti-globalization protestor is perceived to be a 'demo tourist', a 'groupie' who follows these events around the world for the purpose of disrupting them: it is seen to be a lifestyle as well as a political choice.

The trouble is that the mainstream media, politicians, academics, as well as the Antifa, attempt to associate nationalism with extreme violence, especially against immigrants. (To read the German newspapers, one could be forgiven for thinking that nationalists are responsible for all the crime in Germany). We have a long way to go to reversing that image problem. So, any of our demonstrations must be peaceful - despite any provocations by any Antifa or police.

Inevitably, some nationalists will object that students, youth, etc., are too narrow a sub-section of the population, that they are a minority; and that the views of the radical Left (especially the anti-globalization Left) are likewise the views of a minority - the communists, anarchists and the like do not have large numbers on their side.

To respond to the last objection first: As noted before, the communist groups in Australia are not nearly as big as the mainstream political parties. But, compared to the nationalist groups, they are enormous. We nationalists have trouble filling a room with 10 people - and yet we make declarations about taking the country over, expelling all the migrants, etc. The outdated Trotskyists, who go the party-political route and bomb out at every election, and who conduct boring weekly lectures on Marx's Kapital, have more numbers and a more solid following than we do. They succeed in gaining this following because they target students, and their propaganda (their posters, badges, their newspaper (the Green Left Weekly)) is better than anything we can do at the present time - it is hip, trendy, progressive, and in touch with today's political culture.

Secondly, in a liberal democracy, it is minorities, not majorities, that acquire a real following and accumulate the real power. Here I will quote John T. Flynn, an American conservative and author of 'As we go marching' (1944), on the appeal of Mussolini:

I must be careful not to infer that Mussolini did what a majority of the Italian people wanted. He had made one important discovery — a principle that most successful politicians in a parliamentary state understand and that is perceived by few of their intellectual critics. It is that parliamentary societies are not governed by majorities but by combinations of minorities. "Majorities are inert," Mussolini said to his faithful Boswella, Signora Sarfatti, "but minorities are dynamic." He had perceived that society is composed of groups profoundly concerned about their several group interests. They are all minorities. Each minority is far more interested in its special minority objective than in those vague, general subjects that concern the state as a whole. It comes about, therefore, that two seemingly hostile minorities can be induced to unite upon a third proposal of a general nature provided they are each rewarded with a promise of fulfillment of their own special desires.

I can point out plenty of examples from modern politics where this rule applies. For instance, there is the National Party, Australia's agrarian socialist party, which represents a minority economic class that is fast becoming irrelevant, and which, at the same time, has state and federal representation in every state and territory. And then there is the New Left itself - which, in America, recruited enormous numbers among a student class which was, at the time, only 15% of the American population.

I will end by saying that, by veering leftward, at least in terms of our appearance at demonstrations, and in our propaganda, we are staying true to the roots of nationalism. I think it is no exaggeration to say that, were Hitler, Mosley, Mussolini and Degrelle alive today, they would be Freie Nationalisten, or something very much like them.

9

THE TRADITIONAL LEFT FAILED

As we all know, the anti-globalization movement, including the Black Bloc, the assorted strands of communists, anarchists and trade unionists, have failed to stop globalization. If one reads the postings on left-wing (anarchist and communist) message boards on the Internet, the fragmentation of the Left, and the dissatisfaction with the way things are going in the anti-globalist struggle, is apparent.

On top of that, Marx's theory - that the capitalist states are inevitably heading towards Marxist socialism, that the capitalist historical epoch is on the way out and that we stand on the threshold of a new communist era - has been disproved by the collapse of the Soviet Union and the slide of communist states like China and Vietnam towards a free-market capitalism (or at least, social democracy). According to Marx's historical prediction, the collapse of Soviet and Eastern Bloc communism should not have happened, and the decline of communism in Vietnam and China, should not be happening. I know, from my own experience, that the tentacles of globalization have reached even into Vietnam and Laos - one can see Coca-Cola billboards everywhere. Western foreign investment in Indochina may be 'good for the economy' (whatever that phrase means) but, at the same time, its appearance is a depressing reflection of a replacement of a unique Indochinese culture and way of life with a faceless (and raceless) Western, global 'Starbucks' one.

So what went wrong? Here, in this essay, I will be explaining that communism, even before Marx, was flawed from the outset on the basis of its principles. I will also argue that socialism is something distinct from communism, and that socialism, and a socialist revolution (not a communist one) in the West is still possible. I will here be quoting extensively from a classic work by a German socialist historian, The History of the Social Movement in France, 1789-1850, by Lorenz von Stein, originally published in 1850. Stein was a Hegelian and a proto-

Marxist of sorts, and a big influence on Marx. I will be using him as a touchstone because his understanding of communism and socialism predates Marx, and is in much the same language as Marx's, while at the same containing none of Marx's errors. For that reason, he gives a valuable insight into capitalist society, the class relations which exist under capitalism, and the socialist alternative which exists to it.

1. Babeufism

What is communism? The reader will say: 'Obviously, what's contained in the works of Marx, Engels, Lenin, Stalin, Mao and the rest'. Not quite: communism, as a concept, precedes Marx. The first communist theorists and activists appeared in France around the time of the French revolution. The first communist, in modern times at least, was a man called François-Noël Babeuf, who was executed by the French government in 1797. It is in connection with Babeuf's movement that the word communism first appears.

So what is it? Firstly, it is the belief that all men are equal - egalitarianism. Secondly, the belief that the main source of those inequalities is the possession of capital, which economists define as wealth being available for the production of goods and services. Ownership of this wealth, or rather, wealth tied up in means of producing goods and services (means such as land, or factories, or shops, for example) is property. Some - a minority - possess property, others do not. Bill Gates, James Packer, Warren Buffet, Rupert Murdoch and other capitalists possess large amounts of property; others possess only a little (the small businessman, or farmer); while most people possess none at all. The social gulf between the property owners and the non-possessing class is vast: so, in order to bring about true equality, we need to abolish property. The land will be owned (and Babeuf's ideas were intended mainly for agrarian societies) by the people who work on it - all the people.

This is the first stipulation for a communist order. The second is: the equal distribution of goods. Suppose that someone works for x collective farm, and earns an enormous amount of money through his labors (or, if it is a barter economy, an enormous amount of goods?). Or, suppose that he does not consume as much as his fellow workers, and thereby accumulates a large amount of money. After that individual has paid his taxes, and paid for his living expenses, he may still have an enormous amount of savings - after-tax income, capital, wealth. That would make him richer than other people in his commune; and it would no longer be an equal society. Therefore, his wealth has to be distributed, equally, to all other members of the commune; he should only be allowed to keep enough to feed himself, and meet his other expenses, and no more.

Likewise, suppose that a farm, in our communist model, experiences a very large demand for its products in comparison to the other communal farms. That farm would require more laborers than the others; perhaps the laborers on that farm would gain higher status compared to other laborers on other farms. Therefore, in order to enforce equality, laborers have to be discouraged from working on that farm; or consumption of that farm's products has to be discouraged; or both.

The reader will now see the main problem of communism. In order to ensure that everyone gets the same amount of goods for differing amounts of work, a higher authority will have to intervene to enforce equality; likewise, a higher authority will need to intervene in order to allocate resources, like labor, to each farm, to ensure that some farms or individuals do not become 'more equal' than others. So, in order to enforce extreme equality, we wind up with extreme inequality. And this is the fallacy of communism which has made itself felt in every communist society without exception. Early critics of Babeuf and communism saw this straight away - even before the revolution in Russia in 1917.

The early communist program was quite explicit about the levels of control needed to maintain it. In the communist doctrine, individual economic interactions are to be strictly regulated and directed:

Three basic rules for any communistic society are necessary to give public authority the monopoly of the distribution of goods: all private exchange among members of the communistic community has to be abolished;... all products have to be delivered to a public warehouse in order to separate the individual from his labor; and each individual's share of the goods produced must be obtained exclusively from these warehouses by public authorization. These are the necessary prerequisites of a communistic economic order. The fourth rule, the compulsion to work in order to increase the amount of goods to be distributed, is a consequence of the demand for affluence. It may be emphasized or omitted, depending on what type of communism is desired, one of wealth or one of poverty... [Lorenz von Stein, History of the Social Movement in France, 1789-1850, p.167].

All the elements of a Leninist or Stalinist economic system were in place (as I shall explain later) in Babeuf's ideas. Indeed, Babeuf seems to anticipate Pol Pot, who made everyone in communist Cambodia dress the same, took children from their parents and raised them in communal crèches, executed any Cambodian who showed signs of any higher learning, and developed an agrarian militia. Stein writes:

Although the citizens shall be well off, they shall live and dress simply and uniformly. Why have different colors of clothes or different furniture? Why have a well tailored dress for one and a shabby one for another? 'It is essential for the happiness of all individuals that the citizen never experiences the slightest degree of even apparent superiority'. Here communism is already lost in the particulars of clothing regulations...

Even with this complete process of leveling all differences there was one serious danger for absolute equality, namely, the difference in mental ability which manifests itself in the arts and sciences. Here also radical measures were proposed... Lest the unalterable nature of things would reassert the dreaded inequality in the children, education, of course was under no condition to be left in private hands. Only the state was to have the right to educate the children. 'The more domestic education there was the greater would paternal power become'. All children will be placed in a huge institution, and here, without regard to intellectual qualifications, all will receive a simple and absolutely equal education... The whole press was to be kept within the narrow limits of republican principles: any violation was to be severely punished... The economy of early communism was concerned with war and agriculture. Babeuf's doctrine is one of Spartan virtues... [Stein, op. cit., pp. 165-167, p. 169].

It is no wonder, then, that Proudhon wrote: 'Communism is oppression and slavery' (in What is Property?).

Oddly enough, however, many anarchists today are Babeufists, that is to say, communist, by the definition above. The anarchist wants the abolition of property, and power to be given to 'the workers' - or at least, to the employees of private enterprise (including private enterprise on the land). The State, which exists only to uphold the unequal power relations of capitalism, will be abolished, and a mass of decentralized communes, libertarian, sovereign and without property, will take its place. But the question is: how far will each of these anarchistic communes go to enforce equality? One of the enterprises in the anarchist-run towns and villages may be more profitable than another enterprise; one worker may earn more, or consume less, than the others and so accumulate more wealth. The really successful, worker-controlled enterprise may turn into a new Microsoft or General Motors; the really successful worker, a new Warren Buffet. At some point, then, the community will have to intervene and enforce equality. The same goes for achievements in the arts and sciences and the rest - with the really successful scientist or artist earning more prizes and honors, and more money, than the others...

And all of this has nothing to do with The State. That is, the negative side-effects of communism can occur without a State, even though, in anarchist mythology, the bad, 'Statist' communists Lenin and Trotsky perverted the cause of true communism and socialism when they crushed the Soviets, which were, in anarchist hagiography, proto-anarchist communes worthy of emulation. Even without the State, the communist idea entails that people must be crushed to fit the communist ideal of equality, thus bringing about an order which is even more repressive and coercive than capitalism.

2. Marxist communism

The traits of Babeuf's communism carry over into Marx's, as we can see. But, in Marxist theory, the Soviet Union, Mao's China, Castro's Cuba and all the other communist countries were not truly communist. As anyone who is acquainted with Marx's theories knows, history, in the Marxist view, progresses in historical phases. At the time of Marx's writing, mankind was standing on the threshold of the end of the capitalist phase; the next phase was to be followed by a period of 'socialism', which would then be followed by a period of perfect communism, where all men would be equal, everything would be owned by everyone, etc.

Certainly, the Soviet Union and other communist countries were not perfectly communist in that sense; but they were more communist, and more Babeufist, than anything else. Take Stalinism as an example. Some concessions, under Stalinism, were made to individual acquisitiveness - in other words, the individual's desire to accumulate large amounts of money for himself and not to share it with others. As the Australian economist Ian Ward writes:

In Stalinism, material rewards were designed to induce individuals to act in accordance with goals and targets determined by higher authority. Among the distinct characteristics of the reward system was: a heavy reliance on piece rather than time rates [in other words, payments per good produced, rather than payments by hour worked]; extremely wide differentials which reflected not only one's status but the industry or sector in which one worked; the payment of bonuses for overfulfilment of one's target; the payment of high rewards, together with special privileges, such as restricted shops, to members of the party; and an emphasis on the individual member rather than the group as a whole in determining the rewards. By contrast, a more collective form of material incentive was practiced in the group form. Failure to perform was often associated with a negative form of incentive. [Ian Ward, The Soviet Struggle for Socialism, VCTA Publishing, 1992, p. 25].

Having said that, equality, and collective ownership, reigned in Stalin's Russia. For instance: all State-owned enterprises were forbidden to sell goods to one another (a tire factory could only exchange tires with a machine parts factory, for instance). The enterprises used profit as an accounting measure - that is, the enterprises did make profits - but all of these were redistributed back to the State. The collective farms were not owned by the State, but run by the workers on them, who were in turn monitored and directed by State officials. The farms, after producing their agricultural goods for the State, were allowed to keep the leftovers, which were then distributed among their workers (but there was often little left to distribute).

In a previous quotation from Lorenz von Stein, it was mentioned that, under Babeufist communism, four conditions had to be met for a communist society to exist: 1), all private exchange has to be abolished; 2) all products have to be delivered to a communal warehouse; 3) all goods in these warehouses can only be obtained through public authorization; 4) all are compelled to work in order to produce a greater amount of goods, which are then to be distributed to everybody. Every communist State - whether it be Stalin's, or Mao's, or Pol Pot's, or Castro's - works according to these principles. For instance, take 4): the mobilization of the masses to produce more for the community was one of the distinguishing traits of Stalinism:

[Under Stalinism] *a whole range of symbols of social approval and disapproval, as well as mobilization and emulation techniques, were employed. For example, individuals and groups were made model workers or awarded badges, and banners as external symbols of good performance. In addition, all citizens were mobilized either directly through the bringing together of large numbers of people to achieve some specific target or indirectly through massive advertising in the form of slogans on buildings, pictures of successes in public parks or through a media campaign.; 'Catch up with the West' and 'Forward to Communism' were commonly-used slogans. More specifically, emulation campaigns were used to encourage workers to learn by the example of others and work harder.* [Ian Ward, op. cit., p. 25.]

Both Marxist communism, and Babeufist communism, are the one and same thing in practice: communism. And that communism can be reproduced at the decentralized level of the anarcho-communist: we can have a mini-Maoism, or mini-Juchism (Juche being the official North Korean ideology), which is what anarchist-communism and its offshoots are. The anarcho-communists may deny it, but, by necessity, they will be led down the same path, and be forced to abandon anarchism in favor of communism.

From my comments here, it may seem that I believe that communism is entirely a bad thing. But it is not, at least, from the nationalist perspective. After all, recall Stein's phrase: 'The economy of early communism was concerned with war and agriculture. Babeuf's doctrine is one of Spartan virtues'. Such a description reminds me, at least, of certain elements of the German National Socialist, or Italian Fascist ideology, or Evola's Traditionalism. And I must confess that I as a nationalist look at a country like North Korea, or Cuba, with some degree of envy: there, the respective populaces are disciplined, and led, by a political leadership which is anti-US and which, despite all its faults, acts in the national interest as represented by the State - above all classes, all special interests, which exist in our own liberal democratic societies. There are no business lobbies there calling for policies which are harmful to the general well-being as there are here, for instance, and no trade unions doing the same. There is no degenerate phenomena along the lines of 'Chavism' in Britain, and one can be sure that social pathologies are dealt with firmly by the law. At the same time, no-one doubts that Cuba and North Korea are dead and repressive countries, and that their standard of living is far below that of the Western States. The challenge for any theorist of Western nationalism is to isolate the good from the bad.

3. Socialism

So, what is socialism? Stein defines it this way:

All those systems, and all those ideas, which aim at establishing labor's control over capital... and making labor the guiding principle of society, may be called socialist. Socialism is the second blueprint for a social system based on the social idea of equality. Socialism in all its variations is infinitely superior to communism. Its basis is labor, and thereby, individuality, this fountainhead of all true wealth and of all diversification. Socialism does not desire to realize the abstract of equality of men, any more than it desires to eliminate a person's individuality... Socialism does not desire, as communism does, to abolish differentiations among individuals and therewith society and the order of the whole; it aims to build society on the principle of labor independent of property. [Stein, op. cit., p. 85.]

Stein, elsewhere, goes on to outline what he means by social reform, and how it can be achieved:

The major concern of a social movement is not the problem of poverty. The social problem which social reform tries to solve is the result of the laws which determine the relationship between capital and labor and thus also govern society, the constitution and the development of each individual personality... We have shown that the contradiction in the situation of the proletarian consists in his dependence on the property-owner because he owns only labor and no capital... As long as the inherent nature of capital and labor remains unchanged... differentiation and dependence are inevitable. It would be a complete misinterpretation of the nature of social life to consider the abolition of differentiation as the aim of social reform... The abolition of this differentiation is not at all the aim of the proletariat... The proletariat wants to acquire capital. Here is the core of the problem. [Stein, op. cit., p. 92.]

So the solution is, says Stein:

Personal independence in this [acquisitive] society rests on the ability of even the meanest worker to acquire capital. This provides an opportunity for everybody to break through the traditional pattern of social classes and of the ensuing dependence.... As long as this opportunity exists in the form of a rule also extending to the worker, no contradiction is apparent, and the social order is stable, no matter how great are the dependence and the differences between the two classes. The essence of the social question and of social reform in our present society is therefore clearly indicated. The problem is whether it is at all possible, in this acquisitive society, to provide labor with the necessary opportunities and corresponding institutions for the acquisition of property commensurate with the accomplishments and standards of labor. The social reform movement consists of the work, the activities, the suggestions, the attempts, the laws, and the institutions which aim to create these opportunities for the working class. [Ibid.]

4. Socialism and its applications to Nationalism

I think, after the exposition above, that the reader can understand what socialism is and how social democracy, and the social democratic parties (like the German SPD, the British Labor Party, and the Australian Labor Party) are socialist or at least contain socialist elements and aim at social reform. But there is one important change which has occurred since the socialist doctrine was first propounded in the early 18th century. That is what I call the 'blue-collarization' of socialism. 'The workers' in socialist doctrine are, theoretically, anyone without property, i.e., anyone who has to work for a living as opposed to living off rents and dividends. A call centre worker in a phone company like Telstra is a worker, perhaps even a proletarian; the investor who lives off Telstra dividends, or capital gains on sold Telstra shares, is a capitalist. (And, in theory, the CEO whose job it is to manage Telstra on behalf of the shareholders is a very rich worker). But somewhere along the line of the history of socialism, the worker or the proletarian became 'working-class' as we know it today: i.e., a blue-collar. The CEOs, or even the white-collar workers, are not 'workers'.

The difference, I think, between white collars and blue collars is as follows. In the economist's jargon, the blue-collar menial laborer possesses a great deal of 'physical capital'. That capital - the wealth available for the production of goods and services - is the blue-collar's muscle power, which is used to produce goods and services in the sectors of industry he works in. Whereas the white-collar worker relies on 'intellectual capital', i.e., skills which stem less from muscle-power and more from some skill which comes from higher education and training.

It has been stated at the New Right blog, and indeed, in many other places, that German National Socialism, Italian Fascism and their variants in other countries (Mosley's Fascism, for instance), were socialist, all right - but socialism for the workers with more 'intellectual' than 'physical' capital (students and academics fit into that category).

This is not to say that blue-collar workers did not support fascism - they did - but that the white-collars were overrepresented and were its primary support base.

As well as that, small business - the petit bourgeoisie - formed another pillar of the fascist support base. The petit bourgeoisie work for a living; but they own a little more capital than the average salaryman or salarywoman, but much less than a big capitalist.

So the NSDAP was a party of the German worker, all right, but of the worker who had more intellectual than physical capital, or who had possession of comparatively small amounts of capital. (On top of that, the NSDAP appealed to small farmers, in particular, the peasantry). There is plenty of evidence for this in the literature. Martin Broszat, for instance, recounts that the NSDAP appealed to youth, and to the German mittelstand (middle classes):

The share of young voters who found the NSDAP most appealing was particularly high. What attracted them was the Nazi image as a party of youth. There was also the pressure of youth unemployment with its demoralizing impact. In this way young people became politicized at an early age and in turn began markedly to shape the public style of the NSDAP and the SA.... It was in particular young people of traditional liberal-bourgeois or conservative family background who dissociated themselves from their parents' politically and joined the NSDAP.

The main social basis of the Nazi mass movement was therefore the broad spectrum of the Protestant middle class in town and country. As early as 1930, the sociologist Theodor Geiger explained the political landslide of the September elections in terms of a 'panic among the Mittelstand'. He argued that fear of proletarianization was an even stronger motive among large parts of the old and the new Mittelstand than their actual degree of material deprivation. Although objectively, these groups were becoming proletarianized, their anti-proletarian and anti-socialist consciousness which had been molded by their education and social background held them back from voting for the left-wing parties. Instead they began to search for a third way between socialism and capitalism, and it was the Nazis who promised it with their emotionally very effective propaganda extolling the Volksgemeinschaft. Only a few people in the socialist movement recognized at the time that the massive successes of the NSDAP among peasants and the impoverished lower middle classes were partly a consequence of a dogmatic Marxism; for all this type of Marxism was able to offer the panic-stricken 'petty bourgeoisie' and peasants was a 'proletarian class consciousness' against which they had developed a psychological block. [Martin Broszat, Hitler and the Collapse of Weimar Germany, 1984, pp. 86-87.]

The above quotation should be made compulsory for every nationalist in the West - not to mention every Marxist. The fascist movements in Europe in the 1920s and 1930s, whether they were in the Netherlands, Germany, Britain, Rumania, or Italy, gathered their mass support simply because they paid attention to the social classes which were in need of help but had been neglected by Marxism. Nationalists can likewise fill the gap in the West today - especially now, considering that Marxism and communism are spent forces. If we are to advocate socialism, it will be much more appealing than communism, for, as Stein says, socialism, unlike communism, does not aim at a society where no-one earns more or has more than anyone else and where everyone is perfectly equal.

5. Objections

The first objection anyone could make is that, at present, in Australia at least, we are experiencing great economic success, and that, in good economic conditions, the propertyless classes are much less prepared to abandon the 'acquisitive society' and capitalist order. While economic conditions in the West in the 1930s were uniformly terrible, they are not so today. One only has to look at Australian unemployment, for instance, which was 4.3 % in the June quarter - the lowest in over thirty years.

It has been stated here before that the unemployment figures, in Australia, and elsewhere in the West, are kept artificially low using statistical trickery. The opinion columnist Ross Gittins estimates that, once the underemployed and 'discouraged jobseekers' are factored in, the current Australian unemployment rate stands at 9 or 10 percent - hardly the best in Australian economic history. (Ross Gittins, 'Credit where it's due on unemployment', Sydney Morning Herald, February 14 2007). Elsewhere in the West - France and Germany, for example - unemployment is much worse: the official unemployment rates, which underestimate the true extent of unemployment, are much higher than Australia's.

Secondly, there are pockets of deprivation in Australia, even among the workers who possess 'intellectual' capital - for instance, the students. The article 'Extent of student poverty highlighted[2]' makes the claim that many Australian undergraduate and postgraduate students are struggling on less than $A10,000 a year, and are studying with a very high level of personal debt.

As well as that, inflation, as manifested in the rising prices of commodities like oil, is very high at the time of this writing; and central banks in the Eurozone, America, the United Kingdom and Australia have hiked interest rates to high levels - in Australia interest rates are the highest in ten years. The results have not been catastrophic, but have caused some economic hardship, especially to the heavily indebted petit bourgeoisie. It is, then, a time for the electorate to turn leftward, not rightward.

The other objection is, 'What's to then stop Australian voters, for example, from going over to the mainstream, social-democratic Labor Party? Why should they go over to your brand of socialism?'.

Again, I will point to precedents in 20th century history. In Weimar Germany, for instance, the socialist vote was split three ways - between the NSDAP, the German Communist Party, and the social democratic SPD. The NSDAP, in terms of bringing about social reform for its

---

[2] August 8 2007, at http://www.news.com.au/story/0,23599,22208668-29277,00.html

constituency, proved to be a much better party than the SPD, which had been running Germany federally, and at the state level, for years. Likewise, social democratic parties regularly come into office on the Continent and accomplish little. I do not think, either, that the Australian Labor Party will accomplish much in alleviating unemployment after it wins the federal elections this year (if it does win) - although it is conceivable that interest rates and inflation may come down over time.

6. Conclusion

One of the reasons why communists do so well at recruiting students is that hardly any other political group (and that includes nationalists) pays attention to student needs. A recent communist poster around Australian university campuses, for instance, reads 'Abolish student poverty/Abolish HECs [student] debt/No more fee increases'. In the view of the average student, these policies are good policies. The student, on the basis of that, will be more inclined to support the group whether it is communist or not. For the most part, other mainstream parties hardly seem to give a damn.

As Stein would say, all political parties have a class basis. A political idea only makes the transition from theory to practice when it appeals to the needs of a certain economic and social class. And that is the difference between a socialist group and a nationalist one (or at least, nationalism as it exists in Australia). A racist slogan like 'Pakis go home' is not the expression of a social movement; it is an expression of animus, of resentment. But, on the other hand, propaganda which explains why Subcontinental immigration is bad because, among other reasons, it affects the economic well-being of a certain economic class is social theory.

Fascism, in the 1920s and 1930s, had a huge mass base in Europe. After the war, neofascism did not. This cannot be explained wholly by persecution at the hands of Allied-imposed State sanctions against neofascism. The reason why neofascism failed to make headway was that economic conditions were too good in Europe in 1960 or even in 1970. Secondly, the theorists of neofascism (men like Yockey and Evola) failed to ground their politics in a class base, unlike the canny fascist demagogues Hitler and Mussolini. They could not find a socioeconomic group to align themselves to, or at least, had no wish to align themselves to any such group.

Admittedly, economic conditions today in the West are not at the catastrophic level of the 1930s. It is far better, materially, to be one of the propertyless-classes - even one of the lumpenproletariat - in the West than it is in, for instance, Africa or India (which is why so many Africans and Indians are emigrating here). But we should not allow white guilt over our privileges stand in the way of socialism. In the 1930s, Germany, Italy and Japan portrayed themselves as 'proletarian nations' - that is, countries which, even though they had a very high level of industrialization and wealth, were in an inferior position compared to France, Britain and the United States, and were deserving of better treatment in the sphere of international affairs. Nationalists in the West need to adopt the same mentality. We may be members of wealthy nations, and members of the white race, the most privileged in the world; but, at the same time, we deserve social reform, and the system which can deliver it, socialism. And that means reclaiming the word socialism from the Left.

10

THE STRATEGY OF TENSION

Introduction

This article has been written with a view to outlining an overall strategy for nationalist groups to follow – a course of action. In the weeks since the APEC demo, it has become clear to more than a few observers that our communist and militant anti-racist (Antifa) opponents are incapable of debating with us intellectually, and indeed are incapable of intellectual expression. A long, intellectual article posted at the New Right blog will have, in the comments section, abuse and threats of violence from our communist opponents – and never a discussion of the ideas and personages involved (e.g., Babeuf, Stalinist economics, Lorenz von Stein, de Benoist...). And, again and again, we at New Right (as do many other nationalists in Australia, whether they be German or not) get tagged with the 'Neo-Nazi' label – this is despite the fact that we here, at this site, have made our opinions clear on German National Socialism and the phenomenon known as Neo-Nazism (or Nutzism, as we disparagingly call it).

Having said that, the reaction from our communist opponents is, I think, beneficial. It can only benefit our cause, as I shall explain below, and part of our strategy ought to be to continue to provoke similar reactions in the future.

1. What is a Neo-Nazi?

Neo-Nazism is an attempt to revive German National Socialism in the modern era. As we know, German National Socialism was a form of fascism. There are a number of definitions of what fascism actually is, or was. Fascism can be defined as a radical form of socialism for the petit bourgeoisie (Hayek's definition, and the definition of many other free-market conservatives who locate German National Socialism on the Left of the political spectrum, not the Right); or as an attempt to introduce a Traditional order in the modern world (which is how Evola understood it)... What distinguishes German National Socialism from other forms of fascism (Quisling's, Mosley's, Mussolini's) is its adherence to the Führer principle. Simply put, National Socialism needed a Führer figure to hold it all together, and was nothing without him. As the German historian and liberal anti-Nazi Martin Broszat writes:

National Socialism was not primarily an ideological and programmatic, but a charismatic movement, whose ideology was incorporated in the Führer, Hitler, and which would have lost all its power to integrate without him. Hitler was never merely the spokesman for an idea that would have had an equivalent importance and existence without him. On the contrary, the abstract, utopian and vague National Socialist ideology only achieved what reality and certainty it had through the medium of Hitler. Thus there could be no effective opposition against Hitler in the name of the National Socialist ideology. Where this was none the less attempted, as for example by Otto Strasser and his mainly intellectual following, the features of the National Socialist ideology, which were composed of emotions, resentments and dreams, were exchanged for an ideology directed towards concrete material action (which was consistent in that respect and naturally permitted no omnipotent Führer) and failed to appreciate the charismatic foundation of the National Socialist movement. It had been far more typical of the general attitude of Party functionaries from the various ancillary organizations of the NSDAP before and after 1933 that however much they thrashed out bitter quarrels amongst themselves they did not as a rule turn against Hitler, but tried to win him over to their respective interpretations of the National Socialist ideology and program. That is they basically recognized him as the interpreter of the correct 'idea' and did not question his supreme authority to rule on ideological matters too. (Martin Broszat, 'The Hitler State: The Foundation and Development of the Internal Structure of the Third Reich', 1969, p. 29).

So, in order for there to be a Neo-Nazi movement, there has to be a neo-Führer, who takes Hitler's place symbolically as the integrating, charismatic head of the revived Nazi movement. The communist and militant anti-racist opponents of Western nationalism understand this instinctively: which is why, whenever they are on the lookout for a 'Nazi' revival, are always hunting for the 'new Führer', whether he is Dr James Saleam, the 'Reverend' Patrick Sullivan, David Palmer, or Jack van Tongeren.

On the other hand, it could be argued that there can be a 'Führer'-less form of 'Neo-Nazism'. The NPD is accused, by the German and international media, of being 'Neo-Nazi' all the time, even though it has no charismatic 'Führer' figure. In all fairness, the NPD does have a few things in common with the old German National Socialist and fascist movements. For starters, both are mass-movements, which emphasize extra-parliamentary organization; both form women's and children's groups, and other groups which embrace people from all walks of life, all professions, with the intention of being more than political parties; both are on the Left, politically speaking, in many of their social and economic policies; both are radical and uncompromising; both have suffered persecution at the hands of liberal democratic States; both tend to make a mystique of street action and confrontations with communist opponents; both of course, are German and nationalist. One could, on that basis, apply the description 'Neo-Nazi' to the NPD. But, again, there is no Führer, and my argument (and Broszat's) is there can be no German National Socialism, old or new, without a Führer-figure.

One of the problems of identifying the likes of the NPD with 'Neo-Nazism' is that so many other ideological groupings have appropriated parts of the National Socialist doctrine. Do we castigate the Greens, for instance, for being environmentalist, when one of the first environmentalist politicians was Adolf Hitler? A few scholars acknowledge the influence Hitler's National Socialism had on Swedish social democracy – the welfare-statist brand of socialism which, in turn, influenced the British Labor Party (in the 1960s) and the Australian

Labor Party (in the 1970s). In fact, one of the definitions of German National Socialism could be: welfare-statist social democracy plus dictatorship.

Incidentally, one can see how the Führer-as-integrator principle works for other political ideologies. Chavezism, for instance, is inconceivable with Chavez: in that respect, Chavezism is more 'Neo-Nazi' than the ideology of the NPD.

Oddly enough, the communists adhere more to the Führerprinzip, or 'leader principle', more than we nationalists do. Communism, even today, is nothing but a gallery of 'great leaders': Marx, Engels, Lenin, Trotsky, Stalin, Mao, Castro, Che, Ho Chi Minh, Kim Jong-Il, Kim Il-Sung, Tito, lesser lights like Salvador Allende... Their word is law: none of the members of the communist parties are allowed to question the rulings, on any conceivable subject, by these men. Communism is the most authoritarian movement in the history of the world; it is also the most bound up with personality cults, 'Great Leaders' (or 'Dear Leaders'). Hitler and Mussolini, of course, imitated this (and many other parts) of communist doctrine, and German National Socialism could be described as being little more than German Stalinism.

The advantage of the communist application of the Führer principle is that it discourages questioning, thinking and debate. Were the followers of communism allowed, for once, to question where socialism is going, what they, through their activism, are doing to achieve it, what a communist Australia would actually look like, communism would collapse. Or rather, belief in communism would collapse. Socialists would ask, for instance, how it is that mass immigration of Africans, Muslims and Indians helps the Australian working-classes – when these immigrants (especially the more disadvantaged ones, like the Sudanese) would compete with Australians for welfare benefits. And what on earth do gay rights have to do with socialism? Surely capitalism cannot be to blame for discrimination against gays? And why support socialism in Cuba when Cuba uses fierce state repression against gays? There are no answers to these questions: which is why the communist Führer principle is needed. It keeps communists from thinking.

2. What is wrong with Neo-Nazism?

To me, 'Neo-Nazism', particularly in its Nutzi, uniform fetishist form is a bizarre, antiquated and ultimately self-defeating ideology. Enough of it has been said elsewhere at the New Right site.

But, obviously, what I and many other nationalists dislike about 'Neo-Nazism' is not what our opponents on the mainstream Left dislike about it. To them, the objection to 'Neo-Nazism' is simple. During the Second World War (itself started by Germany, when it invaded Poland in 1939), Germany gassed eight million people, using weapons of mass destruction, and threw the corpses into giant ovens. Some were turned into soap; others into lampshades. The horrible, shriveled corpses at Dachau and Bergen-Belsen are testimony to the evil of the ideology of German National Socialism, which committed the most terrible crimes of the twentieth century.

Now, according to the communists and the Antifa, the 'Neo-Nazis' want to bring back that order, and start gassing, not only Jews, Poles, homosexuals and gypsies, but anyone who is not a white European or of European descent. Alan Moore's classic 1988 graphic novel, V for vendetta, offers a good summary of the communist and Antifa view of Western nationalism – and the consequences of a 'fascist' return to power. The graphic novel depicts a dystopian Britain in the late 1990s, where 1930s-style fascists have taken over the world and have killed a good many Jews, homosexuals, Pakistani and Caribbean immigrants in death camps, and like Dr. Mengele, carried out sadistic medical experiments on the inmates. The mainstream Left sincerely believes that propaganda like V for vendetta depicts nationalist goals accurately: they believe that we nationalists are all working together towards the same goal – of eliminating, through death camps, the 'racially impure' (whatever that means) members of Western society.

The Antifa demonize their opponents, making them out to be satanic. Militant anti-racism plays on nothing but fear: it is pure emotion. And it is purely negative, as well: ask them what their political policies are on inflation and interest rates, for instance, or conscription or abortion or the death penalty – and they have no answer. Because of the lack of foundations, the lack of arguments, they can only appeal to fear. They are more a belief-system than a political ideology, and with their appeals to fear and irrationalism, plus the almost religious attribution of satanic qualities to their opponents, they resemble a cult, like the Raelians or the Scientologists.

In the Antifa and mainstream ideology, the New Right and the National-Anarchists are part of the same 'Neo-Nazi' conspiracy. A few individuals of the mainstream Left have expressed their trepidation that naïve youths (who have been insufficiently indoctrinated, i.e., not converted to Marxist-Leninism) may go over to the National-Anarchist side, not understanding that the National-Anarchists are 'Neo-Nazi' fakes. In the communist scenario, the naïve youths, after becoming members of a National-Anarchist group, will eventually be led down the path to 'Neo-Nazism'. Possibly, the new National-Anarchist recruit will be brought to a secret cavern by the other members, where he will find framed portraits of the Führer and George Lincoln Rockwell, and swastika flags, on the walls. The secret 'Führer' of the movement shall doff his anarchist garb to reveal a homemade brownshirt uniform. He will then unveil a fantastic plan to take over Australia and build death camps, run by blonde, Nordic women in 'Ilse the She-Wolf of the SS' uniforms, and fiendish doctor-sadists like Mengele.

Regardless of whether or not one believes in a National Socialist gassing of eight million people, the interesting thing is that the communists have a long backlog of atrocities of their own to atone for – and they do not apologize for them. While many nationalists push a revisionist line, the communists do not. Confront a communist with the nine million Russians killed by Lenin and Trotsky – during the Red Terror, and the mass famine deliberately triggered by the Bolsheviks to pacify the Russian population – and he will shrug and regurgitate the old Leninist cliché that 'One cannot make an omelet without breaking eggs'. Then there is Mao, whose Great Leap Forward killed 18 to 34 million people (depending on whose figures you believe); Pol Pot; and lesser-known figures like the Ethiopian communist Mengistu Haile Mariam. Even Castro, who is fondly regarded by Australian communist groups, killed thousands after his takeover of Cuba.

My point is that, given communism's track record, people ought to hold communism's past atrocities against Australian communist groups like Socialist Alliance, Socialist Alternative and others. How do we know that these groups do not have a secret plan to collectivize Australian agriculture, and starve millions of Australians to death? Will Australian soldiers be rounded up, Khmer-Rouge style, bound with nylon ropes and have their necks broken with blows from pick handles? (Or perhaps they will be given the softer, North Vietnamese communist version: internment in a 're-education' camp until they get their thinking straightened out?). And what of the capitalist class? Will the Packer family be liquidated on the spot, or will they be forced to work with their hands (for the first time in their lives) in the fields of our newly-collectivized farms, while communist overseers, wearing black pajamas and carrying Kalashnikovs, jeer at them and curse them? ('No rice for you today, Mr. Packer! Work harder!').

3. The reality

I am, of course, being facetious here. The Australian communists do not have the demonic drive of a Lenin, Mao, Ho Chi Minh, Castro, Pol Pot, Mengistu: they do not have what it takes to bring about a revolution.

Even more important is the fact that no communist revolution has come about by the revolt of the working classes against the capitalists. All the communists in history have won power as a result of war. Lenin won power only after Russia's catastrophic defeat, at the hands of Germany, in WWI; the Bolsheviks emerged from the ashes of the Russian Civil War as the most powerful and unified force, and took advantage of the subsequent chaos to impose a dictatorship. Likewise, every subsequent revolutionary owes their successes, not to mobilizing the working classes, but from defeating their opponents on the battlefield. (One exception is Mengistu: but Mengistu came to power through a military coup, and was able to use soldiers to liquidate any bourgeois-liberal, monarchist or rival communist opponents).

The truth is that the old-school communist revolutionaries had a unique genius, lacking in today's Western communist parties, for exploiting the political opportunities that arose as a result of chaos. That chaos is not present today, and it is unlikely that today's communists would know how to harness it to their advantage.

And so today's Australian communists, who are schooled in the theory, but not practice, of communism, naively believe that power will be theirs for the taking, once the inevitable downfall of capitalism gets going. Marxist theory proves, scientifically, that the capitalist mode of production will go the way of feudalism – into the dustbin of history. All the communists have to do is agitate at the universities and TAFEs (by selling the Green Left Weekly and trying to encourage students to attend pro-Chavez rallies), march at trade union anti-Work Choices rallies, and run in elections. Then revolution will come about. Australia will turn into Cuba, except it will be a Cuba where people of all sexual orientations will be free to do their thing…

In truth, the only communists to hold true to historical communist practice are a few isolated groups around the world who have taken up the path of armed struggle. The Maoists in Nepal, who adhere to a Pol-Potist ideology and are engaged in an off-again, on-again war against the Nepalese State, are classic, old school communists. Given the disarray of Nepalese politics, it is not inconceivable that the Maoist revolution could succeed, and a handful of revolutionaries could end up imposing their will on a reluctant and hostile Nepalese population. Naturally, however, such conditions are not likely to replicate themselves in Australia.

4. What to do

Unfortunately, much confusion exists among nationalists as to who our enemies are. Nationalists tend to speak of 'the Left', and lump together all the disparate factions of the Left into a single group: 'lefties', 'crusties' and the like. But the fact of the matter is that the communists, and the anarchists, for instance, are unaware that we nationalists exist – at present. The only faction of the Left who are aware of us, and consider us to be a serious threat, are the Antifa, the militant anti-racists – who strive selflessly to avert a second Holocaust by posting photographs, names, addresses, telephone numbers, etc., of nationalist activists on the Internet.

It should be mentioned that it is doubtful that the Antifa are really 'Left' at all. Although they adopt a Trotskyist rhetoric ('smashing fascism' is a Trotskyist phrase), they do not seem to support communism or anarchism – nor even the watered-down social democracy of the Labor Party. No, they believe in racial harmony and the brotherhood of man – and the use of violence to enforce it. They believe in the same pan-racialist, multi-racialist ideology as the Labor Party, or the Democrats, or the Greens – but, in their case, they make that ideology political. Schmitt defines the 'political' as any conflict that is raised to the level of war between two or more parties: and certainly, the Antifa are political by Schmitt's definition. But they are not Left, and, in Australia, they are not do not possess the numbers, the discipline and the organization of the European Antifa. (According to postings on Stormfront, European nationalist activists are disappointed by the caliber of the Australian Antifa. Indeed, the Antifa in the Netherlands, for instance, is so powerful that it controls neighborhoods, and hides illegal immigrants who are being sought by the police there). Here, their warfare is psychological. They could not summon up the numbers needed to 'smash fascists' at an APEC or anti-Work Choices rally; the communists, however, can.

The point, though, is that the communists are not aware of us. They do not acknowledge we exist, and to them, we are an irrelevancy. After all, history is inevitably progressing towards communism: does not the hostility of the Australian electorate towards Work Choices show this? We nationalists do not fit into the grand scheme of things. To the communists, nationalists are 'Nazis', and 'Nazism' was a tool of the German capitalist classes, who sought to lure the German working-classes away from communism. The capitalist class of Australia, however, is not, at the moment using 'Nazism' and 'Fascism' to trick the Australian working-classes; it is using the Australian Labor Party. Fortunately for communism, the Australian proletariat will eventually wake up to the Labor Party. The upshot is that communists and other like-minded progressives need not pay any heed, for the time being, to the 'Neo-Nazis' of New Right and other nationalist groups.

Were they to notice us, however, their reaction would be along the lines of: the 'Neo-Nazis' of New Right, National-Anarchism and other nationalist groups are in the pay of the Australian capitalist class and possibly the federal government itself. These 'Neo-Nazis' are trying to lure the Australian working-classes away from their salvation, communism. Really, all capitalism is 'fascist, racist, imperialist' – 'Neo-Nazism' is capitalism with the mask torn off. The solution? 'Smash fascism', use violence, use any means necessary...

The communists can be expected to say many things along these lines, and no doubt they will end up alienating potential members (e.g., left-leaning university students) with their hyperbole and bellicose rhetoric in attacking us; they will also, inadvertently, generate more publicity for us than we could manage to achieve ourselves. It is also possible that, by doing so, they will succeed in making us more attractive to the politically uneducated (that is, not indoctrinated with Trotskyism) university student.

I will, at this point, digress and bring up the subject of Hugo Chavez, and in particular, one of the techniques he uses to get attention for his ideas. Recently, Chavez announced that he plans to bring his 'Bolivarist revolution' to Venezuelan high schools, and alter the content of high school text books along 'Bolivarist' lines, filling them up with the crapulous mumbo-jumbo of communist and other progressive ideologues (including the Colombian guerrilla groups). The reaction to Chavez' announcement was entirely typical. Liberal democrats, in Venezuela and the United States, reacted with outrage, and demanded that Chavez adhere to the norms of free speech and liberal democracy. Chavez' supporters (and he has many) reacted with enthusiasm.

Nowhere did anyone declare that Chavez' policy was well-intentioned, but needed to be examined more closely, etc., etc., in the way that the Labor Party, for instance, reacts to any of John Howard's policy announcements. No: Chavez polarizes people, he splits them down the middle. You either love him or hate him. But this is precisely what Chavez wants. He wants the liberal democrats, the Bushophiles inside and outside Venezuela, to hate him; and he has, over many years, become awfully good at it. He instinctively knows what to do in order to get his opponents frothing at the mouth, hurling invective and hyperbole, making themselves look foolish, and piquing the interest of the otherwise apathetic masses. And he has done this, not once, but many times; he is, to a certain extent, a one-trick pony, pulling off the same stunt again and again. His opponents have such little regard for him that they do not see how they are being manipulated by the master. The solution to Chavezism? Incorporate him into the system, and treat him with respect: hold press conferences with him and George Bush, where the latter defers to him as respectfully as he would to Ehmud Olmert or Ariel Sharon.

One can see the parallels with Australian nationalism: all the communists at APEC had to do, for instance, was to invite the National-Anarchists up on stage and ask them to speak; the audience would have listened respectfully, and applauded – just as they did with the indigenous Australian woman at the start, and the North American conscientious objector – and National-Anarchism would have been neutered.

This will never happen. The communists can be expected to react with hostility and hyperbole, every time; and the same reaction can be provoked every time. In that sense, they are as predictable as machines.. The communist policy is always the same: no platform for fascists! No free speech for Nazi scum!

So how do we provoke them? How do we get their attention? Well, we only need to repeat APEC a thousand times over – APEC with more and more permutations. But it is essential to keep up the 'Left' talk, the 'Left' symbolism, the 'Left' imagery, the 'Left' sloganeering', and the 'Left' methods of mass organization, mass activism, extra-parliamentarism, and anarchistic, non-hierarchical, decentralized organization. Such an approach will ensure that the communists will work themselves up into a state of hysteria: we are using their symbols, their ideas, to lure the naïve young away from progressive, multiracial, tolerant communism and towards 'Neo-Nazism' and capitalism. They will be unable to help themselves, and unable to see that the best means of 'smashing' us would be to give us equal rights and equal time at their rallies, and possibly in their publications as well.

The Australian communist groups appear to recruit using what I call 'chaff-cutter' methods. They attract literally hundreds of young Australians, mainly students. But many of the prospective new members are naïve about the communism of a Socialist Alliance or Socialist Alternative: they believe that these organizations are liberal, like the mainstream political parties – that they encourage free thought and free debate. But the prospective member learns, very quickly, that Lenin and Trotsky had, in advance, worked out the answer to every political problem in existence – and that he had better recognize this or ship out. Subtle, and then not so subtle, peer pressure is used to bring a recalcitrant into line. Eventually, the prospective member gets fed up and ceases his association. He is a liberal and an individualist – both traits fostered by our liberal democratic society – and, at the same time, like many idealistic young people, wants to do something good and progressive. But the inflexibility which lies at the heart of any Marxist-

Leninist party, and which is communism's greatest strength (and greatest weakness) repels him.

The scenario is not all bad, however, for the communist group: a small minority of the prospective recruits will stay on and the communist group is left with a small hard-core. Communism is, above all, a ruthless ideology, which often turns on its own (there is no need to cite the many examples from history). But their recruiting and indoctrination policies – more reminiscent of a cult than anything else – get results. The wheat is separated from the chaff.

Here, though, we nationalists can step in – and pick up the chaff. And, it has to be said, we are not going to expand as a movement by recruiting the same old faces from Stormfront Down Under – the same old white nationalists and Australian bush patriots who have been hanging around the nationalist scene for years and years. No, we are only going to expand by recruiting people who have a fresh perspective which comes from being on the outside of the existing nationalistic scene.

In this connection, it is advisable that nationalists go out and attend as many political meetings as possible: lectures on Lenin, Trotsky, Chavez, etc., delivered by Socialist Alliance, Socialist Alternative, and Resistance. But not only political meetings of the left; nationalists should attend also meetings of the mainstream parties like, here in Australia, the Liberal party, the Greens, etc.

The best course of action is to go there, as normal, intelligent people, and ask questions about their beliefs, and try and engage them in the debate they are so averse to. This is a New Right Australia strategy.

5. Mistakes made

Recently, a nationalist friend of mine – a man with a long and distinguished career in Australian nationalist activism – showed me a nationalist publication which he had helped edit and publish. It was a handsome production. But, while looking through it, I found a caricature of an African immigrant – a giant African immigrant, stalking the streets of some Australian city, with a knife in his hand, and, needless to say, up to no good. I chided my friend for inserting such a crude caricature with overtones of old-fashioned racism: it could have come straight off Tom Metzger's website. My friend joked, half-heartedly, that at least the cartoonist didn't draw blood dripping from the African's mouth. I rested my case.

On the back of the publication there was a reproduction of a beautiful painting, done one hundred years ago, of the inauguration of the first Australian federal parliament. Looking at the picture, I found myself confused as to who the intended target audience of the magazine was: monarchists? Old Australian types who voted for Menzies in 1949? Often this Australian nationalism is an emotional nationalism, with no intellectual foundations, no ideology. Ask them to define what an 'Australian' is, and they will have no answer.

Even if one is not a republican, one will find such imagery incongruous. Granted, governor-generals are part of Australia's past: but the emphasis is on the word past. Any young person (and the only people who could revel in such patriotic Australian imagery must be very old indeed – at death's door if they voted for Menzies, anyhow) would find such a nationalist publication off-putting – as dull as a school trip to a museum of Australian history.

As for the cartoon of the African – and there were similar crude caricatures throughout the magazine – there are other, more tasteful ways to address the question of immigration. Link immigration to globalism, for one; or point out how immigration drains Australia's resources (e.g., water resources) and is bad for the environment... No need to use pictures of blonde, Nordic women cuddling blonde, Nordic babies, either.

Oddly enough, I agreed with around 90% of the publication's content: the difference between their approach, and New Right's, was one of emphasis, and of imagery. Thinking it over, I saw that the whole problem could be summed up in the form of a parable.

Suppose that Henry Lawson, or Jack Lang, or some other Australian 'bush' socialist could be transported in time to 2007. We nationalists would explain to him that the old Australian Labor Party, which championed white working man's racialist socialism, has ceased to exist; in its place is a party of namby-pamby multi-cultism. The union movement, too, is no longer interested in fighting immigration: all it wants is the abolition of Work Choices and federal and state Labor governments. Indeed, the union movement has lost the political power it once had – only 17% of the Australian workforce is unionized. The way forward for socialism – for a system where labor dominates capital, and not the other way around – is to restructure the entire political and economic system. That means changing liberal democracy. But that goal, in turn, can only be achieved by building up a mass movement on the streets, which will bring about radical change through mass pressure. To build a mass movement, we need to bypass the unions and the political parties, and start taking our message – of racialism and socialism – directly to the masses. What's more, we need to talk the language of today – not the language of 100 years ago.

Unfortunately, our way is, for the moment, blocked – by communists, who, like parasites, attach themselves to every progressive cause, whether it is anti-globalization or the trade union struggle for better wages and conditions. They are unpopular, in the minority, and they adhere to a theory which has been falsified by history. But they are convinced that their cause is the only moral one, and every political ideology contradictory to their own (including ours) is evil and immoral, and should be destroyed, by violence if necessary. Their bark is worse than their bite, but they are still numerous enough, and hostile enough, to prevent nationalists from reaching the masses and becoming a true, mass political force. And so one of the prime necessities of our movement is to unblock the communist blockage…

And that is what I would tell Henry Lawson.

In relation to this, it should be asked: why, if the communists have been going at it for so long, are they so unsuccessful? The communists enjoy all kinds of advantages that we nationalists do not: the media coverage they receive is generally favorable (e.g., see the media coverage of the APEC demonstrators); they can display their names and faces with impunity (at least, they will not be treated as harshly as a so-called 'Neo-Nazi' nationalist); they have numbers, nice newspapers, propaganda fliers, badges, flags, banners… And they can attend any demonstration for any cause whatsoever – anti-globalization, anti-Work Choices, anti-war – without being set upon by the other demonstrators. And, furthermore, most of Australia seems to support their positions on, for instance, the war in Iraq, or Work Choices (or perhaps it is the case that the communists attach themselves to popular causes). And yet, they have made little to no headway in all the years they have been here: the communist revolution is further away than ever, and they cannot get one MP elected to state or federal parliament…

The answer, or the beginning of an answer, came to me when I was leafing through old issues of the Australasian Spartacist newspaper from the 1970s. This is a long-running Trotskyist-communist newspaper, which began in 1973 and which is still running today. More or less, it makes a cult, a fetishistic cult (like the Nutzi-cult of Hitler), out of Trotsky and Lenin: every political event – from the war in Iraq, to a trade union dispute in Sydney, to a scuffle between two rival communist groups holding stalls at a university – is interpreted from the perspective of Trotskyist Marxist-Leninism. The frightening thing is that there is no difference between the writing style, and ideas, of the 1970s issues written thirty years ago, and the issues written today. This raises the possibility that the same person has been writing all the articles for that newspaper all along – and getting nowhere. This obsessiveness, and the refusal to countenance anything other than an orthodox Leninist and Trotskyist view of socialism and politics, makes me speculate that the authors of Australasian Spartacist, and other communist publications (like the Green Left Weekly) are literally insane.

And this is why the communists have been failing in Australia for so many decades: they cannot ditch Lenin and Trotsky. It is not that Australians do not want radical socialism; it is that they cannot understand what two dead Russians – who died a long time ago – have to do with a political struggle in Australia today. (The same could be asked of many nationalists today: why is Hitler, for instance, so important?).

6. Conclusion: The strategy of tension

Something else that leapt out of those old issues of Australasian Spartacist was an account of the famous 'Battle of Lewisham' in Britain in 1977, which was an epic confrontation between the British National Front and hundreds of communist protestors in South-East London. The clash was violent, leading to hospitalizations, and the police use of tear gas, riot shields, etc., against the protestors. Reading the venomous account of events from the communist perspective, I was reminded of the (far smaller, by comparison) Battle of APEC. Economic, and to a great extent, social, circumstances in Britain in 1977 differed from those of Australia in 2007: but otherwise, nothing has changed. The National Front in the 1970s was a mass-movement with a popular base, and left-leaning; it won a certain amount of support from the British working-classes, effectively challenging the communists and socialists in what the latter two regarded as their own domain. The communist response was to 'crush fascism'. Hence, the ensuing confrontation at Lewisham.

Perhaps (depending on whose account you believe) some members or supporters of the National Front, who were still bourgeois in outlook, and still held to liberal democratic ideas, found the idea of a political confrontation with communists off-putting; that is, they did not want to suffer verbal abuse from communists, and have bricks thrown at them, and be assaulted. This is a natural enough reaction. But they did not realize, and many nationalists in Australia today do not realize, the political value of these confrontations. Suppose that 500 or a 1000 nationalists from all around Australia joined up to march through Sydney or Melbourne. The police would be out in force, as would the media; and so would the communists. The spectacle would ensure more media coverage for nationalism than we could generate by ourselves (through pamphleteering, etc., or through websites); and, at the same time, events would radicalize our membership and draw them closer to one another. And the communists would do all of this for us for free. If we are to look at it in economic terms, the return from a demonstration pays even more than the investment in pamphlets and websites.

And all of this can be done tomorrow. Some liberal media commentators will argue that events like the Battle of Lewisham came about because of the high inflation and high unemployment in Britain in the seventies; which is untrue. All one needs is a large body of nationalists who are prepared to go out and demonstrate: then the communists will show up, and behave like they have behaved for the past ninety years. Like monkeys in a zoo cage, they will jump up and down, shriek and spit. And the average Australian will wonder what all the fuss is about, and some of them may even become interested in nationalism as a result.

The essential thing is this: all demonstrations have to be well-organized, for a worthy cause, and above all, disciplined!

We at New Right do not endorse violence. One can, however, use the metaphor of war: that is, any confrontation with communists is a battle in a political war. A good many nationalists in Australia and elsewhere are in political fairy-land; they think they can form a nice little bourgeois liberal democratic party, and be treated with the same respect, and enjoy the same rights, as all the other liberal democratic parties. But, once their parties get up and going, they are due for a shock. The communists will use non-liberal democratic means to deny them their rights. And, possibly, a more effective Antifa will spring up and oppose them with the same means.

Christian Blocher's Swiss People's Party (SVP) recently held a rally which was set upon by the Black Bloc of Left-wing Chaotics (an Antifa Black Bloc), who caused an enormous amount of property damage and disruption. The group was arrested, and the rally went ahead. Christian Blocher's party posted a triumphant account of events at http://www.svp-udc.ch/internet-tv.html. But Australian nationalists cannot expect to get off as lightly. This is why we must take the war (again speaking metaphorically) to the enemy.

And, while I am not a militarist, I must state my belief that this kind of confrontation is good: it cleanses, it purifies, it bonds the 'soldiers' – who are made up of disparate social groups who may have otherwise never have come into contact with one another – together. And, psychologically, to go on the attack is much better than going on the defense: which is the posture many nationalists take now, confining their 'activism' to the Internet and not trying to get their ideas out to the Australian community. This is why we at New Right Australia/New Zealand endorse a strategy of tension. And we endorse direct political confrontation, with the goal of smashing political dogmas, and forming a real social alternative.

11
THE TYRANNY OF INDIVIDUALISM IN A LIBERAL DEMOCRATIC SOCIETY

Introduction

This is an article divided up, roughly, into two halves. The first concerns liberalism, or what liberalism has become. It details a transition in liberalism – from a cult of elections and parliaments, to a cult of doing your own thing (even if that involves sexual and other debauchery). The second half outlines what I consider to be the New Right antidote to the poison of modern liberalism, and explores some of the ideas of a liberal democratic anti-intellectual, Karl Löwenstein, who, in 1937, wrote a paper describing some of the political techniques used by the fascist political movements of the time. Some of those techniques are still being used by nationalists around the world (Hungary, Sweden, Russia, Britain, etc.), and, in my opinion, we in Australia can apply them equally as successfully here.

What is liberalism really?

Nowadays, one can read, in the Western liberal democratic press, daily denunciations of General Musharaff of Pakistan and the Burmese Junta. The two dictatorships have attracted media attention recently because of their flagrant crackdowns on 'liberal democratic' political opponents (or at least, opponents who the Western media assumes are liberal democratic).

Now and then, other dictatorships and/or authoritarian regimes will occupy the spotlight. One recent case is Georgia, which is led by an American-backed liberal democrat, Mikhail Saakashvili, who came to power through an 'Orange Revolution'-type coup (nicknamed the 'Rose Revolution') in 2003, but is now in danger of being overthrown, and now, as a result, has declared a state of emergency and is using state repression – including tear gas and rubber bullets – to subdue the populace.

A perennial target of the Western media is Vladimir Putin. Despite his massive support among the Russian people, and massive election results in his favor, the Western media still considers him to be 'undemocratic' and 'illiberal', and upholds his critics – small groups of 'liberal democratic' dissidents, who have no popular support, and no agenda beyond being anti-Putin – as being more 'democratic', and certainly more morally worthy.

So we have a collection of countries – Burma, Pakistan, Fiji, Russia and others – which are manifestly illiberal and democratic in the eyes of Western liberal democrats. But what is it, exactly, that makes our liberal democracies so good? Why are they preferable to these dictatorships and authoritarian regimes? The answer is, simply, that people in liberal democracies are 'more free' – in fact, they are 'free to do their own thing'.

To explain: One of the objections the Western liberals have against Iran is that supposedly Iran (along with other conservative Islamic States) imposes a strict dress code upon women. Women are allowed to dress freely in the West, as well as engage in nude sunbathing and the like: part of that, in my view, is because of the Western cultural heritage (particularly in the northern European countries) which traditionally has given more freedom to women compared to, for instance, the Mediterranean cultures of North Africa and the Middle East. But according to the liberals, this freedom has nothing to do with the West and its cultural heritage, but is, or at least should be, universal. What is more, that freedom should be forced on to countries with a low regard for the freedom of women, and even on ones (like South Africa or Papua New Guinea) with a high incidence of rape. Israel is held up as a model to other Arab nations – 'the only democracy in the Middle East' – because of, among other reasons, its high degree of personal freedom (which translates into a thriving gay and ecstasy culture). Such a level of freedom is 'Western'. Consistent liberals, however, will acknowledge that liberal freedom cuts both ways: a recent article in the British

Guardian newspaper denounces the fact that the secularist regime in Tunisia encourages harassment of women wearing the hijab and men wearing beards.

A country needs more than a high level of personal freedom to qualify as a 'democracy' in the eyes of the West, of course. For one thing, there must be a separation of powers: the executive, judiciary and legislature must be separate. And, as Carl Schmitt would say, there must be debate: all legislatures must go through the farcical process of debating the pros and cons of each piece of legislation before the members vote on it (even though the passage of each bill is determined, well in advance, along party lines). The Israeli parliament, the Knesset, allows plenty of debate, all right – mostly on the topic of how best to kill, starve or drive out the Palestinians, or who to bomb first (Iran or Lebanon or Syria?). Because of the daily debates in the Knesset, Israel qualifies as a 'liberal democracy'.

On top of that, there are other requirements: elections, a multi-party system...

These days, however, there are many countries which do have elections, and an ostensible multi-party system, which are still condemned as 'un-free' and 'un-democratic': Russia, Belarus, Iran, Syria, Egypt, Tunisia, and Venezuela. The Western liberals claim that the governments of these respective countries repress the political opposition, fail to hold elections which are completely, 100% 'free and fair' (that is, meeting the Jimmy Carter electoral observer-standard), reduce the legislature to a rubber stamp, and censor journalists. The worst thing about these countries is that they do not see changes of government: an opposition party is rarely, if ever, voted in: so they are de facto single party States. So, then, these countries are situated in the hazy no-man's land between complete dictatorship and complete liberal democracy. (And even pro-Western countries like Singapore and Malaysia fit into this category). Some are worse (or better) on the liberal democratic scorecard than others: Russia and Syria tolerate opposition political parties more than Saudi Arabia and Iran – just barely. In many cases, e.g. Russia, Belarus and Iran, a real opposition exists. In other cases, e.g., Venezuela and Egypt, there is a political opposition which does win seats in parliament, but suffers from repression.

Again, though, we have to ask: what is all this freedom for? Surely elections, multi-party systems, frequent changes of government, the freedom of the press to snipe and criticize the government of the day, parliamentary debates, cannot be an end in themselves? Was Iraq invaded to give the Iraqis these dubious blessings? No: the answer is that the Iraqis were not free, as the Israelis are (or as Americans are) – not free to be gay, for instance, or drop ecstasy pills, or consume pornography, or to cross-dress. The Iraqis, and the Iranians, must reach the lofty status of Israel, which sent a transvestite singer to the Eurovision song contest – and won. Ahmedinejad attracted much Western condemnation for his insistence that 'There are no gays in Iran' (a mistranslation: he really said that there is no gay culture in Iran like there is in the West). The most strident criticisms against the Iranian political system is that it is run by Mullahs (democratically elected or not) who 'repress the rights of women' and repress gays.

This freedom occurs within a context, a structure, of course: in the West, and in Israel, the consumption of drugs like ecstasy is not legal, or de facto legal. It is merely widespread and socially acceptable – the outcome of a liberal society. (Whereas the consumption of heroin and ice, on the other hand, is not socially acceptable). It is fine to use drugs like ecstasy, marijuana and cocaine, or be a homosexual, or dress as a Goth or an Emo, or for a man to dress as a woman, so long as it does not harm others (to the extent that the consumption of ice and heroin does). If women are to be allowed to dress immodestly (immodestly in comparison to Iranian standards), this does not stem from traditional Western freedoms granted to women, or from tolerance of nudity, but from a woman's universal right to freedom of self-expression.

Some countries are more socially conformist than others: Japan springs to mind. Ironically, America, up until the 1960s, used to be a very conformist country. One only has to look at the films from that time, the fashion magazines, newsreel footage, to see this. Francis Parker Yockey wrote on this topic in Imperium (in the chapter 'America', under the heading 'World outlook'). The passage is lengthy, but is worth reproducing here in its entirety:

Every American has been made to dress alike, live alike, talk alike, behave alike, and think alike. The principle of uniformity regards personality as a danger and also as a burden. This great principle has been applied to every sphere of life. Advertising of a kind and on a scale unknown to Europe is part of the method of stamping out individualism. Everywhere is seen the same empty, smiling, face. The principle has above all been applied to the American woman, and in her dress, cosmetics, and behavior, she has been deprived of all individuality. A literature, vast and inclusive, has grown up on mechanizing and uniformizing all the problems and situations of life. Books are sold by the million to tell the American "How to Make Friends." Other books tell him how to write letters, how to behave in public, how to make love, how to play games, how to uniformize his inner life, how many children to have, how to dress, even how to think. The same principle has been extended to higher learning, and the viewpoint is nowhere disputed that every American boy and girl is entitled to a "college-education."... A contest was recently held in America to find "Mr. Average Man." General statistics were employed to find the centre of population, marital distribution of the population, family- numbers, rural and urban distribution, and so forth. Finally a man and wife with two children in a medium-sized town were chosen as the "Average Family." They were then given a trip to New York, were interviewed by the press, feted, solicited to endorse commercial products, and held up for the admiration of all those who fell short in any way of the desirable quality of averageness. Their habits at home, their life-adjustments generally were the subject of investigation, and then of generalizing. Having found the average man from the top down, his ideas and feelings were then generalized as the imperative-average thoughts and feelings. In the American "universities" husbands and wives attend lecture courses on marriage adjustment. Individualism must not even be countenanced in anything so personal as marriage... The men change from felt hats to straw hats on one certain day of the year and on another certain day discard the straw hats. The civilian uniform is as rigorous— for each type of occasion— as the strictest military or liturgical garb. Departures from it are the subject of sneers, or interrogation [...]

All one can say is: how things have changed. America is now the land of the non-conformist, in every way in which Europe was supposed to be. In Europe in the twentieth century, the cultivation of one's personality – i.e., emphasizing one's differences from the rest, one's eccentricities – was always tolerated, if not encouraged. (The one exception is Nationalism: if you are a nationalist, and against multicultism, you are a Nazi, fascist, racist, bigot, etc., etc).

Non-conformism was part and parcel of the European aesthetic and intellectual tradition. America, though, had always resisted this – being the land of the conformist, the 'square', the 'average man'. That was until the 1960s. I would hazard that the main cause was the shift in American popular culture. In the fields of music and film, the role of the individual genius, in revolt against society's norms, came to the forefront. Even the films like Top Gun and Flashdance, which embody the ethos of the conservative 1980s – supposedly a return to traditional 'American values' – celebrate the heroic, non-conformist individual. There are still plenty of 'average Joes' depicted in American popular culture, but the protagonists of television shows like Desperate Housewives and House are eccentrics – the 'average Americans' are background characters.

The odd thing is that this attitude of individualism, eccentricity and non-conformity has filtered through to the American (and Western) population at large, and, in the end, has become a new kind of conformity. Everyone has to be different: the subsumption of oneself to a group, or a higher ideal, or to anything besides one's own individual desires and preferences is an offence against the liberal spirit of the age.

And it is this individualism which lies at the heart of modern liberal democracy. A country like Germany may be only barely liberal democratic – with its State control of the media, its repression of nationalists and Holocaust deniers, its thousands of political prisoners. In this, it is not so different from a country like Egypt or Tunisia. But where Germany is genuinely liberal democratic is its parliamentary debates, its multi-party system – and its tolerance of ethical hedonism and individualism. One cannot wear a 'fascist'-style political uniform: that would be 'Nazi'. But one can prance around, high on drugs, in a strange costume, at the Berlin 'Love Parade', a kind of annual Mardi Gras event where the attendants openly consume party drugs like ecstasy – while the police turn a blind eye. (In Singapore, or Belarus, it would be a different story).

Freedom and degradation

My own views on this are as follows. Freedom to take drugs in public, or for gays to marry one another, or to dress 'differently' (i.e., dress like Paris Hilton, Britney Spears or Lindsay Lohan) are low on my list of priorities. Freedom to take a revisionist view of German history, and the history of the Second World War, or to criticize immigration, are, on the other hand, very high. My view is that if that freedom is not possible, then other freedoms are not worth having at all. From my perspective, Russia is more free than the West. Russia, like the West, makes the Allied-Communist interpretation of the Second World War, part of its State ideology; but, unlike the West, it is indifferent to those who disagree with the government's line on those subjects. Russia does not persecute people who take an alternative view of the history of WWII; and it could not care less if Russian nationalists oppose immigration. A German with a long history of nationalist activism, like myself, can walk the streets of Moscow a free man; but is in danger of arrest if he visits his own country.

Regarding the other freedoms – which my liberal democratic countrymen prize so highly – I am largely indifferent: the consumption of drugs, liquor, pornography, etc., have been part of civilization ever since it existed; likewise, individualism, the right to act 'crazy' or different', is part of European culture and history. (One only has to look at the Weimar Republic, with its cult of drugs and individualism. Because of the lack of individual identification with the community and the State, the Republic fell apart; out of the ashes arose the Third Reich).

But a recent incident has forced me to reconsider my views. Recently, I took a holiday in the United States, and, while in San Francisco, happened to be in a main street where a local, American version of the German 'Love Parade' was passing through. As in Germany, the revellers were high on drugs, prancing around to music, and wearing outlandish clothes. Being a good tourist, I started taking photos on my digital camera. I then saw, out of the corner of my eye, a grossly overweight, middle-aged bearded man, entirely naked except for a pair of sneakers. He had shaved all the hairs off his body (except for the hairs on his face), and, judging by his even tan, must have been a frequently-practicing nudist. I then became aware that he was masturbating – openly, in front of everyone. I must admit I was completely taken aback. Thinking that no-one back home would believe me, I took photos of the man. He looked up, saw me, and continued to masturbate – and even struck poses. Finally, he finished doing what he was doing. Another of the attendees – another overweight person, this time a woman, dressed in strange attire (somewhat reminiscent of a Viking costume) – came up and hugged him.

The man clearly must have been on drugs: ecstasy, fantasy, ice, goodness knows what. The essential thing is, it dawned on me that: this is the 'freedom' that George W. Bush speaks of; that he defends; that he insists on imposing on other countries through the unilateral use of military force. Liberalism has changed: from a doctrine of pluralism (manifested through a multi-party electoral system, parliamentary debates, a free press giving dissenting views) to a doctrine of complete individualism free of any restraints.

The liberal argument now is that individuals should be given the maximum amount of freedom, and be allowed to do what they like, so long as those people are not 'hurting others'. With this principle in mind, the Netherlands allows the smoking of marijuana; it also allows gay men to organize sex parties. Unfortunately for the Dutch liberals, the principle was challenged recently, when it was revealed that gay men, infected with AIDS, would lure young men to these parties, drug them with a date rape drug (called, appropriately, 'Easy Lay') and inject them AIDS-infected blood. This caused a scandal.

But, presumably, the liberal position is: organizing sex parties is OK; gays should be allowed to do what they like; they only cross the boundary between right and wrong when they hurt others – and injecting men with AIDS-infected blood is 'hurting others'. The same principle applies to the revellers in the San Francisco Love Parade: the revellers high on drugs, masturbating publicly in the nude, were not 'hurting others'. There may be laws on the books against indecent exposure, and the consumption of party drugs, but these are written by prudes, moralists, 'wowsers' (as the Australians like to call them). It's OK for people to let their hair down once in a while and break those minor laws. Why not let people be free individuals and do their own thing? What is wrong with that?

Freedom and Tradition

The answer is long and complex. I will give it as follows.

Evola, in his work, gives an outline of the various kinds of spiritualities, as they have appeared in human civilizations: he identifies, following Nietzsche, a 'Dionysian' spirituality, which is a spirituality of shamanism - achieving altered states of consciousness through the use of drugs, alcohol and revelry. Evola has ambivalent views towards 'Dionysianism': on the one hand, he believes that it is an attempt to reach a mystical state of being which is truly 'Traditionalist'; on the other hand, he thinks that is a mindless, debased spirituality, which breaks down all barriers, all hierarchies – between the sexes, between the classes, between all ethnic groups. What is more, 'Dionysianism' is a feminine spirituality – which explains the frequent association of the god Dionysos with female worshippers and revellers. Evola, of course, has nothing against femininity: merely the feminization of men. Evola's preference, as his readers know, is for the 'Olympian', 'Solar', 'Apollonian' spirituality, which is 'virile' (from the word viros, meaning male).

Now, all this is rather metaphysical: but Evola was a nationalist philosopher, or at least a philosopher of a kind of nationalism which many nationalists today are sympathetic with. Certainly they reject 'Dionysianism', or at least, the debased elements. And clearly, in my view, the phenomena of the Love Parade, and the behavior I saw there, fits into the category of 'Dionysianism'. As a New Rightist, then, I must reject it. Evola writes of the 'lunar' spirituality, which rejects hierarchy and authority, and regards all men as 'one' – no matter their race or social position. Certainly, the self-debasement of the Love Parade fits into that category too.

And it is a small leap from the 'lunar' spirituality of the Love Parade to the ideology of the Antifa. The Antifa objects to nationalism because that ideology draws distinction between races, and refuses to acknowledge the non-Western immigrant as being the equal, and deserving equal rights, as the indigenous Westerner. The Antifa accepts the immigrant, and the gay, as 'brothers'. The stereotype of the 'Lefty' or 'Crusty' is someone who wears his hair in dreadlocks, Rastafarian-style, to show his affinity with the Negro, and smokes marijuana, which, as anyone who has tried it knows, is a notoriously egalitarian drug (which makes one accepting of all people and all things).

All rather complex and metaphysical, true: but Evola's descriptions get right to the heart of things. He was an eloquent man; not surprisingly, he was a poet as well as a philosopher, and could be described as the 'poet of fascism'. No-one managed to put the tenets of that ideology in clearer terms than he did.

New Rightism in action

All of this raises one question: what is that we from the New Right offer, precisely, which is in contrast to the individualism of the Love Parade and George W. Bush's America? It is all very fine to talk of he nationalist's affinity for 'Olympian' spirituality – one can be as 'spiritual' as one wants – but how does it manifest itself in our actions?

As part of the research for this article, I have been looking at a number of film clips of nationalist rallies on YouTube, from Hungary, Rumania, Russia, Italy, Sweden, Britain, and Greece. Despite the national differences, a number of similarities emerged. (These similarities were even present in the film clips from different times: I watched one of National Front demonstration in the 1970s, and one in 2007).

One writer who identified those core elements is an American political scientist, Karl Löwenstein, who wrote a classic article, 'Militant democracy and fundamental rights', in the 'American political science review', volume 31/no. 3, 1937. The article is one of the most influential ever written: it consists mainly of recommendations for a series of 'anti-racist', 'anti-fascist' laws (against wearing uniforms, 'defaming ethnic groups', etc.) which have been put into practice by Germany, France and a number of other Western countries which have sought to clamp down on resurgent 'fascism' and 'Neo-Nazism' in their midst. It ought to rank as the holy scripture of the Antifa movement: except that Löwenstein preaches the state repression of nationalism, not in the name of multi-cultism, but of liberal democracy. But I will not dwell on this side of the Löwenstein doctrine, important as it is, here. I will instead quote a number of things he has to say on the subject of 'fascism' (loosely defined). In my view, he could almost be speaking of nationalism today. He remarks on the surprisingly international character of fascism:

A closer transnational alignment or "bloc" of fascist nations, a "Union of Europe's Regenerated Nations", a fascist International of the multi-colored shirts, is clearly under way, transcending national borders and cutting deeply across historical diversities of traditionally disjoined nationalisms. The modern crusaders for saving Western civilization from Bolshevik "chaos" – a battle-cry which in all countries gone fascist has proved invaluable – for the time being sink their differences and operate jointly according to a common plan. Under this missionary urge, which is one of the most astounding contradictions of a political system based on the superiority complex of each individual nation, what exists of distinguishing marks in program, ideology, and nationally conditioned premises of Realpolitik shrinks to insignificance [...]

He writes, disparagingly, that:

Fascism is not a philosophy – not even a realistic constructive program – but the most effective political technique in modern history. The vagueness of the fascist offerings hardens into concrete invective only if manifest deficiencies of the democratic system are singled out for attack. Leadership, order, and discipline are set over against parliamentary corruption, chaos, and selfishness; which a cryptic corporativism is substituted for political representation. General discontent is focused on palpable objectives (Jews, freemasons, bankers, chain stores).... In brief, to arouse, to guide, and to use emotionalism in its crudest and its most refined forms is the essence of the fascist technique for which movement and emotion are not only linguistically identical [...]

So how precisely does the 'fascist technique' work? Löwenstein writes:

Concomitantly, the movement organizes itself in the form of a semi-military corps, the party militia or private army of the party. Under the pretence of self-protection, the original nucleus of the personal bodyguard of the leaders, and of the stewards for the maintenance of order in meetings, is developed into a large fighting body of high efficiency equipped with the fullest outfit of military paraphernalia, such as military hierarchy, uniforms and other symbols, and if possible arms. Again, this technique has strong emotional values and purposes. In the first place, mere demonstration of military force, even without actual violence, does not fail deeply to impress the peaceful and law-abiding bourgeois. Its manifestation, so alien to the normal expressions of party life, is, as such, a source of intimidation and of emotional strain for the citizens. On the other hand, while democratic parties are characterized by the looseness of their spiritual allegiance, the military organization of the fascist parties emphasizes the irrevocable nature of the political bond. It creates and maintains that sense of mystical comradeship of all for each and each for all, that exclusiveness of political obsession in comparison to which the usual party allegiance is only one among many pluralistic loyalties. When party allegiance finally transcends allegiance to the state, the dangerous atmosphere of double legality is created. The military routine, because it is directed against despised democracy, is ethically glorified as party of party symbolism which in turn is part of the emotional domination. Disobedience towards the constituted authorities naturally grows into violence, and violence becomes a new source of disciplined emotionalism. The conflicts with the state – unavoidable when this phase of active aggressiveness is reached – increase the common sentiment of persecution, martyrdom, heroism, and dangerous life so closely akin to legalized violence during war. In addition, the movement is, within its own confines, genuinely democratic. A successful roughneck forwith rises to distinction in its hierarchy [...]

The quasi-military structure and attributes of fascism are one of its distinguishing features:

The uniform has a mystical attraction also in avowedly non-militaristic countries. The effect of military display on the "soft" bourgeois is all the more last because he contrasts the firmness of purpose of accumulated force in fascism with the uncontrolled fluctuations of normal political life. In politics, the only criterion of success is success. Fascism has been irresistibly successful in other countries; thus far, it has never met with a reverse. In any democratic country, be it traditionally ever so sober and balanced, the existence of a political movement organized as military force makes the average citizen uneasy and creates the feeling of restiveness which emotional politics needs [...]

He then goes on to list a few more of the 'essential techniques', and lists means of combating fascism through legislation:

All democratic states have enacted legislation against the formation of private para-military armies of political parties and against the wearing of political uniforms or parts thereof (badges, armlets) and the bearing of any other symbols (flags, banners, emblems, streamers and pennants) which serve to denote the political opinion of the person in public. These provisions – too light-heartedly and facetiously called "bills against indoctrinary haberdashery" – strike at the roots of the fascist technique of propaganda, namely, self-advertisement and intimidation of others. The military garb symbolizes and crystallizes the mystical comradeship of arms so essential to the emotional needs of fascism [...]

That 'militarism' is applied, by the fascist, as follows:

Political strife carried by the fascists to the extreme of organized hooliganism made the fundamental right of assembly more or less a sham. Creating disturbances in or wrecking meetings of opposing or constitutional parties not only proved a favorite test of the fighting spirit of militarized parties ("meeting-hall-battles" – "Saalschlacht"), but also deterred peaceable citizens from attending meetings of their own selection. The task of the police to keep peace and order at meetings and public processions became increasingly difficult. The ordinary criminal codes being wholly insufficient to curb the deliberate tactics of extremist parties, more stringent legislation was introduced in Czechoslovakia, Great Britain, and proposed in Switzerland [...]

Löwenstein describes the method of the 'provocative march':

A different problem arose when it became obvious that fascist demonstrations, processions, and meetings were held in districts where they could be considered only as a deliberate provocation because of the hostility of the bulk of the people living in these quarters. If, in such cases, disturbances occurred, they were actually created by the opponents. Exploiting this situation was one of the favorite methods of rising fascist methods whereby they could stand on the constitutional right of free processions and assembly [...]

He details, interestingly, the use of the weapon of 'political abuse':

Overt acts of incitement to armed sedition can easily be squashed, but the vast armory of fascist technique includes the more subtle weapons of vilifying, defaming, slandering, and last but not least, ridiculing, the democratic state itself, its political institutions and leading personalities. For a long time, in the Action Française, the finesse of noted authors like Daudet and Maurras developed political invective into both an art and a science. Democratic fundamentalism acquiesced, because freedom of public opinion evidently included also freedom of political abuse, and even malignant criticism was sheltered. Redress had to be sought by the person affected through the ordinary procedure of libel, thereby affording a welcome opportunity for advertising the political intentions of the offender [...]

In an unintentionally amusing passage, he takes note of the distinctly fascist method of using martyrs to exalt one's cause – and dubious martyrs at that:

More patently subversive is fascism's habit of publicly exalting political criminals and offenders against the existing laws – a practice which serves the twofold purpose of building up the revolutionary symbolism of martyrs and heroes and of defying, with impunity, the existing order. It is still remembered that Herr Hitler, in August, 1933, when the rowdies of his party murdered, under particularly revolting circumstances, a political adversary in Potempa and were sentenced to death by the court, proclaimed his "spiritual unity" with them. Only Czechoslovakia and Finland have provided against this practice of morally aiding and abetting the political criminal [...]

Fascism as technique?

At first, when I read Löwenstein's article, I was somewhat offended by it – in particular, by his characterization of fascism as being mere 'technique', not a real ideology. After all, fascism attracted many intellectuals who gave fascism a well thought-out philosophy, an intellectual basis. And certainly, the post-war 'neo-fascist' writers – Yockey, Thiriart, Evola – gave fascism a real intellectual grounding. But, the more I thought about it, the more I saw that Löwenstein's contention was true. After all, it has to be admitted that nationalism – which Löwenstein would classify, rightly or wrongly, as 'fascist' (and certainly his followers in the Bundesrepublik do) – is vague. What the liberal democratic media calls 'policy detail' has never been our strong suit. We are not used to contesting in elections, like the mainstream liberal democratic parties, and, when we do, we do not produce budgeted, carefully-crafted plans to improve children's health care, combat global warming, fix petrol-price gouging, etc., like the Labor and Liberal parties are doing at this Australian federal election. Part of this is sheer lack of experience and money – whereas the mainstream liberal democratic parties have plenty of both, and are very good at organizing the logistics of elections.

New Rightism, more than anything else, is an 'action' movement, not a 'talking' movement, and the heart of our policy, if not worldview, lies in our day to day living: living in community, working in the community, transforming it through our actions.

Nationalism, of course, does tend to elevate people who have fallen in battle – either through actual military conflict, or in the context of a political struggle – into martyrs. Of the film clips I saw, one was a commemoration of a Swedish nationalist martyr – Daniel Wretström, a 17 year old Swedish nationalist killed by immigrants; the other, a wreath-laying ceremony in Hungary commemorating the country's servicemen who had fallen in WWII.

The ultimate historical fascist martyr figure is, of course, Horst Wessel. There is a scene in 'Triumph of the Will' where assembled National Socialist personages sing the song Horst Wessel Lied, accompanied by the inevitable salutes and giant banners: the camera focuses on Göring for a few moments, and one can see the beginnings of a tear forming in the hard man's eye. Without a doubt, nationalists – whether today in Greece or Hungary or Russia, or yesterday in France or Germany – rely heavily on emotion. These emotions are: indignation, against our liberal democratic and communist enemies; a feeling of the rightness of the cause; self-sacrifice; self-abnegation (which comes from service to a higher goal)... All of this is transmitted through formalities and ceremonies: the Swedish nationalists, for instance, put on a candle-lit vigil and procession for the young Wretström . Whereas, in a liberal democracy, the Berlin Love Parade has replaced the torchlight processions of the SS: individuality takes the place of community as an object of veneration in the Bundesrepublik.

Even liberal democrats have to admit that, compared to the political street theatre of nationalism, their brand of conventional politics is mundane. There is nothing in mainstream conservatism, social democracy, environmentalism, liberalism, etc., to compare with it. There is a real pleasure in being part of a crowd of demonstrators, marching past communists who are swearing, spitting, jeering, singing communist anthems, who are being held by mounted police (as in one of the old National Front film clips). It is a peculiar pleasure, to be sure, and not for everyone. But once one has a taste of it, one becomes addicted. I am often chastised by liberal democratic friends, and I have plenty of them, for being part of the so-called 'Neo-Nazi' nationalist scene: I retort to them, 'What am I meant to do? Join the Liberal Party, attend boozy functions, sit among fat, middle-aged men in suits, and listen to speakers like Tony Abbott and Peter Costello drone on about the unions?' The mainstream liberal democratic parties do not give anyone much of a scope for real political activism. What they are about is power to political parties but not the people they claim to represent. New Rightism, on the other hand, is activist-based: and it has the potential to encompass nearly all spheres of life.

One other advantage of nationalism is that it is virtually indestructible. The National Front imploded after reaching a peak in the late 1970s: but it is still in action, albeit with reduced numbers, and this time demonstrating against Islamic immigration and gay marriage. Certain of the problems afflicting Britain have changed, but others remain the same. The prime example of nationalist indestructibility, though, is Germany and Eastern Europe. The Allies and the Soviets embarked on a campaign of unprecedented genocide against Germany and its Allies – with the intention of eliminating 'fascism'. But nationalism has grown back. Part of the reason for nationalism's success is that, being a technique, it is easy to apply in all manner of times and places.

So why do some nationalist movements in some countries grow and others do not? I am biased on this. My belief is that, if the British nationalists, for instance, invested as much time and effort in constant, round the clock demonstrations – and taking the 'war' to the enemy, the communists and Antifa – as they do in trying to win council seats, they would achieve better results (and certainly earn themselves more media notoriety that way). The Internet has proven to be a boon to nationalism, but it has also made nationalists stay at home – preventing them from going out, mixing with other nationalists on group activities (like hiking trips), meetings, conferences and the like, and engaging in demonstrations and rallies.

The demonstration is really at the heart of nationalist 'technique'. Demonstrations are a public show of power: they are political street theatre. What matters in a demonstration is force, strength. Large numbers are required – and flags on poles to make the nationalist crowd look larger than it really is. Loudhailers, loudspeakers mounted on cars, whistles, drums (the National Front in the 1970s made effective use of drums), etc., are all important for drowning out the hateful cries of the enemy (with their inevitable boring chant of 'Nazis out!'). It becomes a pitched battle between the nationalists and the communist counter-demonstrators: and the biggest and loudest crowd wins.

I myself recognize the supreme importance of this: and the importance of getting as many nationalists and New Rightists as possible to attend a demonstration, and take the blows directed at them by the communist enemy. But nationalists, it has to be said, spend too much time on doctrinal disputes. On the National-Anarchist and New Right mailing lists, for example, there was a recent debate on whether or not 'New Right' and 'National-Anarchism' were appropriate names for our ideas. Should we not look for alternative names? Alternatives were suggested: e.g., 'New Left" (the affiliate of the New Right in Portugal actually calls itself 'New Left'), 'New Reason' instead of 'New Right'. One of the objections to the use of the term 'New Right' was that it may be confused with the Anglo-Saxon neo-liberal movement of the same name from the 1980s (as if the average man can remember back that far). As for 'National-Anarchism', are not nationalism and anarchism mutually exclusive concepts?

All of this is somewhat missing the point. The early fascist activists cobbled together an ideology which was 'Left' as well as being 'nationalist': no doubt it confused a good many people. A typical response would have been: 'I can't tell if you people are Left or Right: your ideology is an incoherent mish-mash'. (Some commentators characterized German National Socialism, when it first appeared, as 'conservative Marxism'). I am sure that Mussolini's movement started off without a name: and that finally, at some point, someone felt that they had to give their rather loose collection of ideas a proper name, and someone came up with 'fascism'. But what is in a name? And why do political ideas have to be consistently 'Left' or 'Right'? Political theories, in my view, are not mathematical proofs, where every step proceeds logically from the other. The essential thing is to go out and do. The trouble is that the liberal democratic system wants the Left and Right to fight one another; it is happy with the Left-Right divide; it likes the simplicity of the concepts; it does not want people to think; rather, it wants them to be conditioned, to categorize themselves as green or socialist or conservative. That way, a person only sees himself in terms of that category: the ideology does the thinking for him. Which is why Greens feel that they have to fight nationalists, despite their similarities: Bob Brown and the Green Party have ordained that nationalism is evil, racist, and has nothing to do with environmentalism; so the individual ends up not thinking for himself, and instead obeys his party leaders and the dictates of the mainstream political consensus.

What to do

Sometimes, when I look at the hostility nationalism generates – from the 'militant democratic' governments of Germany and France, in particular – I wonder why it is these governments are so afraid. Look at the footage of any nationalist march, and all you will see – in the last analysis – is a large group of men and women carrying flags and banners, walking along a road. But, from the way the liberal democrats and communists behave, such activities are heinous, and must be stopped by any means necessary. Nationalism will lead to a second Holocaust, etc., etc. (even when the marchers are British or Russian). My pragmatic response, though, is: so what? A bunch of people are marching down the street, waving flags with old Teutonic and Celtic symbols on them – what harm does it do? I wonder what would happen if the German government banned the prohibition of uniforms or Holocaust literature. Would mass riots and discord ensue? Would the Bundesrepublik cease to exist overnight? Simply because 'fascism' in the 1920s and 1930s became a Europe-wide movement, embracing millions of men and women, is no reason to believe that it will happen again. The pettiness and stupidity of the 'militant' liberal democrats expresses itself in actions like the withholding of two years worth of mail to Ernst Zündel, for example.

Having said that, laws come, and laws go (Holocaust denial in Spain has just recently been legalized again) and there is no body of legislation in existence anywhere which has succeeded in shutting down nationalism completely. The Russian nationalists wear masks and uniforms at their rallies, and use the Roman salute; they also engage in paramilitary training, and even own their own Kalashnikovs. The Italians, on the other hand, labor under the same restrictions as the Germans: but that does not stop them from putting on large demonstrations. It is all a matter of working around the Löwenstein-style laws.

The main strength of our movement is our organization – our ability to mobilize large numbers of people for mass action. This, of course, occurs only under optimal circumstances – we waste a good deal of time debating doctrinal differences among ourselves, instead of going and doing what we do best. No doubt the demonstrators in Sweden, Hungary, Russia and other countries have, as individuals, a number of doctrinal differences with one another: but the main thing is that they were sufficiently united, and organized, to take to the streets in defiance of communism and militant anti-racism. Ideally, I would like political activists from all over Europe to converge on London – in particular, the financial district (the City of London) – for an annual pan-European anti-capitalist march. And if police and the media, and the communist enemy, descend en masse upon the march, all well and good. That will garner the attention that we need. Because of the location, we would be sure to get worldwide English media coverage, which is considerable.

The main thing which is holding us back is wrong thinking – and lack of courage, or at least, an unwillingness to offend bourgeois proprieties. One German poster, at a mailing list I frequent, wrote recently:

The so-called "free nationalists" are only free from responsible behavior. They mimic American dress codes and copy antifa strategies which basically makes them appear as dangerous, violence-prone hooded hoodlums. If you disguise your face you not only have something to hide - you also won't garner any sympathies from the populace...

That is a common fallacy among some nationalists. The fact of the matter is that the German populace has been trained to hate all forms of German nationalism; the same goes, to a milder extent, for the rest of the world. They are conditioned, Pavlov-style, to react with disgust. Non-German nationalism in the West is fast going the same way – that is, our liberal democratic masters in the media, the church, the parliament, the trade union leadership, the university, are training the Western masses to find it nearly as equally as abhorrent. The notion, then, that this hatred (and that is what it is) can be done away with by aping bourgeois manners, is wrong.

Related to this is the fact that many people – especially young people – like outlaws and rebels. You can appeal to more people by trying not to appeal to anyone at all, by being yourself and by making your own values in contrast to the norms of the society you live. In popular culture, this fact has been known at least since the 1950s: James Dean, Marlon Brando, and Elvis Presley were marketed, deliberately, as moody, dangerous rebels – and all three of them made fortunes as a result. Many rock bands nowadays are still being marketed as being rebellious as the Rolling Stones or the Sex Pistols. Although rock and roll rebellion has now become something of a tired old cliché, the youngsters never seem to get tired of it, as we see with the continuing popularity of the likes of the EMO cult. Almost everyone understands this, except for the nationalists who are desperately trying to look respectable and liberal-democratic. Instead of acting independently and doing what has to be done, they are more concerned about what the apolitical consumer orientated Zombies thinks about, and trying to appease them.

Other nationalists have described their reluctance to refer to the Antifa enemy as precisely that: the Antifa. Why? Because if the Antifa are anti-fascist, it implies that their enemies – us – are 'fascist'. And we can't have that. I am surprised that Australians, of all people – a people who wrested this country from the Aborigines, and built a country and a State literally from the dirt, facing great personal hardship and struggle – are afraid of a mere word.

To conclude: what we in the New Right offer is an alternative. Löwenstein is quite right when he says that 'fascism' is a method, of confrontation – and investing the political struggle with an honor, dignity and nobility (although he would not use those words). At the risk of sounding 'irrationalist' or 'anti-intellectual', we New Rightists have to make use of the method (and I am stressing the word method) and get to work – the time for talking is over. We have to show the world our anti-liberal alternative – our alternative to the tyranny of individualism in a liberal democratic society.

12

THE PARIS HILTON SYNDROME

This article concerns something that receives little attention from nationalists: celebrities and popular culture, and their influence on both our liberal democratic system and our consumerist society. More specifically, it concerns the role of women in our liberal democracy and popular culture. This subject matter is very much part of our lives: one cannot avoid the celebrity trash gossip magazines, American TV shows, and the role of prominent women in our liberal democracy (such as Hilary Clinton). Moreover, our economy relies, to a great extent, on both consumerism – especially a consumerist lifestyle promoted heavily to women, through advertisements and celebrity culture – and female labor.

From a political view, does any of this matter? Do the antics of Paris Hilton, Britney Spears and Lindsay Lohan matter? Did Princess Diana matter? A person with an old-school, left-wing point of view would say, 'No'. The fetishisation of celebrity women in our culture is a symptom of the fetishisation of capitalist consumer commodities. Once capitalism is abolished, the only women who will appear in advertisements, films and the like will be female communist role models – factory workers, rice paddy farmers, mothers bearing socialist babies and the like.

After the advent of the New Left, the analyses – of images of women in a capitalist society, as expressed through popular culture – became a little more sophisticated. The stern Soviet and Maoist bromides became somewhat old-fashioned, and the neo-Marxists argued that there was something deeper going on.

Here I will be taking an approach similar to that of the New Left – but will be drawing upon Evola instead of Marcuse. Bill White, before his Nutzi phase, used to write some intelligent articles. One of them was on the subject of women in American popular culture, and used some Evolian concepts. (Unfortunately, it is no longer available on the Internet). Evola, I think, is a thinker who is the most suitable for this sort of thing. After all, many of his 'spiritual types', or 'races' (as he defines them) possess masculine and feminine characteristics. In essays like 'Do we live in a gynaecocratic society?' (1936), he said nearly all there is to be said on the subject. The present article will add little to the discussion – much of what Evola has written has yet to be surpassed – but the articles from the 1930s and 1940s are lacking in that they are out of date. They appear dated because Evola did not live in our age – the age of Angelina Jolie, 'Buffy the Vampire Slayer' and the Hilary Clinton presidential campaign bid.

1. Evola's spiritual types

Evola's work, as readers familiar with him know, defines a number of spiritual types, which are known to us through myths, religious texts, folklore and the like. Evola believes that these contain metaphysical truth – and that the task of the Traditionalist scholar is to interpret them. He regards descriptions of ancient events in the Bible, for instance, as history which is literally true – that is, accurate descriptions of the metaphysical states of affairs.

Evola often begins his narratives of 'metaphysical history', of the various ages of the metaphysical development (or, in his view, degeneration) of man, by positing a primordial 'solar', 'Uranian' spirituality, which is followed, in time, by the appearance of 'Demetrian', 'Titanic', and 'Amazonian' spiritualities (among others). It is the Amazonian spirituality which we shall first examine here.

The Amazonian spiritual type represents an interesting combination of both male and female spirituality. To Evola, Amazonian is both a reaction and a transmutation. 'Demetrian' spirituality is feminine, maternal, egalitarian, pacifist, collectivist – the closest there is to modern day pagan worship of 'Mother Earth' and the New Age cults. (Possibly, there is a link here to modern environmentalism as well). In contrast to this, there is the coarse 'Titanic' spirituality – cruel, masculine, militarist, phallic (in a purely physical way) and forever seeking after the higher, spiritual state as represented by the 'Uranian' and 'solar' spirituality. (There are several myths of giants and other demonic races who sought to attain the 'solar' spirituality by force – by storming Mount Olympus and so forth – and being punished by the

Gods for their impudence). Amazonianism is a reaction against the coarseness of the Titanic spirituality, and is a defense of the virtues of Demetrianism. In Evola's narrative of metaphysical history, the two rival spiritualities – the ultra-female Demetrian and the ultra-masculine Titanic – clashed, and produced a feminine spirituality which was not quite one or the other. Amazonianism is feminine, all right, but has taken on assertive, masculine and warrior characteristics. (Evola, of course, has nothing against militarism and the warrior: only the expressions of militarism without a higher, 'solar' spiritual aspect. The militarism of the Titanic spirituality is militarism devoid of any transcendent spirituality: it is the use of force only to attain purely material goals).

This Amazonianism is prevalent today. As Evola writes:

The woman often asserts her primacy in new 'Amazonian' forms. Thus we see the new masculinized sportswoman, the garconne, the woman who devotes herself to the unilateral development of her own body, betrays the mission which would be normal to her in a civilization of virile type, becomes emancipated and independent and even bursts into the political field. And this is not all. ('Do we live in a gynaecocratic society' (1936), translation copyright © 2003 Thompkins and Cariou).

2. Amazons go pop

One can say that those tendencies identified by Evola in 1936 continued into the modern age. Indeed, to look at the popular culture of the last ten or so years, we can say that we are living in the age of Amazonianism. Women warriors abound: killer cyborgs, fighter pilots, deadly martial artists, female soldiers… One only has to think of Lara Croft, television shows like 'Xena: Warrior Princess', the remake of 'Bionic Woman', 'Buffy the Vampire Slayer', 'Battlestar: Galactica' (in which every single female character is an Amazon of some kind), 'Dark Angel', films such as 'G.I. Jane' (a 1997 film which was a portent of the future), 'Kill Bill', 'Charlie's Angels'… Even Guinevere, a more

Demetrian figure, was reinterpreted as a bow-wielding Amazon-type in the 2004 film, 'King Arthur'. (Of course, there are plenty of films and TV shows from the recent past with women warriors – there is 'Barbarella' (1968), the sixties British TV series 'The Avengers', the seventies version of 'Bionic Woman', Sigourney Weaver in 'Alien' (1979) and its sequels, the Afro-American kung-fu heroines of the seventies Blaxploitation films, the Linda Hamilton character in 'Terminator 2' (1991). There is also the multitude of heroines in American comic books. But it is only recently – in the past ten or so years – that the Amazonian woman warrior has reached the forefront).

Now, I am not such a prude that I dislike all American popular culture. I have enjoyed at least a few of the above films and TV shows. But the striking thing is their unreal depiction of women. A reviewer of 'Charlie's Angels' (2000) at the Vanguard News Network site acerbically noted that the film simply wasn't real: no amount of martial arts training, and psychological 'positive thinking', could give women the physical strength to overpower a man in a fight – it simply doesn't happen. They do not have the strength, or the aggression. He cited an anecdote of an incident he witnessed in a parking lot, where a man was berating a woman for her poor driving manners. The woman was twice the man's size, but put up with the man's tirade and nodded meekly before climbing back into her car. In a 'Charlie's Angels'-type universe, she would have, of course, given him a roundhouse kick or thrown him over her shoulder in a judo manoeuvre.

We all know from real life that female aggression is the exception and not the rule. War is a man's business, and it is men who do most of the fighting (and dying) on the battlefield. True, there were female communist soldiers in the Vietnam War, and in the Soviet Union's so-called 'Great Patriotic War': but again, these are exceptions.

So why is it, then, that women are, in today's action-based films and TV shows, increasingly depicted as flying fighter jets, kickboxing, shooting, breaking necks, etc., like men? Why are there women who are portrayed as having inhuman physical strength – a strength which exceeds that of the male characters (e.g., the superwomen in 'Buffy', 'Xena', 'Battlestar', 'Bionic Woman')? They are often shown bending steel bars, terrorizing hapless male characters, and engaging in protracted martial arts contests with other warrior/killer women – all the things that men, or at least the men in the absurd pop fantasy world, should be doing.

Popular culture is all about fantasy – a character like James Bond, who is a connoisseur of fine wine, food and clothes, a great lover, a successful gambler, an unbeatable action hero – appeals to male fantasies. Possibly, the new wave of women warriors appeals to female fantasies. That is, the women who like these films and TV shows have wanted to do these sorts of things, but now, under the aegis of feminism (which teaches that women can be equal to men in every way), they can see those fantasies put up there on the big (or small) screen.

Nationalist writers who have touched upon the subject usually blame it on a conspiracy – a conspiracy, by the writers, directors and producers of Hollywood, to turn women into men, to masculinize them. Usually these analyses are couched in white nationalist terms: the white race is dying, and needs more children; but, because of feminism and other modern ills, white women are not reproducing enough.

Western popular culture, which is tremendously influential, certainly encourages 'feminist' childlessness. One can think of a few of the female warrior characters mentioned above who do have children – e.g., the Uma Thurman character in 'Kill Bill' – but childlessness, and the absence of the comforts of the hearth and home, are the rule. The women characters lead a transient life of adventuring, and children, husbands, mortgages and homemaking only serve to get in the way. (A hit single from the 'Charlie's Angels' soundtrack was, appropriately enough, titled 'Independent Woman').

Whether or not white women are staving off pregnancy, in order to imitate the feminist pop icons, is beside the point. Likewise, it is beside the point whether or not white women should be bearing as many children as possible (and Evola would be vehemently against that notion). The point is that we are seeing an eruption of Amazonianism. Why?

Many white nationalists would blame it on the ethnicity of the group which controls Hollywood and the American TV studios, record companies, etc. – this group, they charge, wants to 'Destroy the white race' through promoting feminist childlessness, and race-mixing. Evola's interpretation, in contrast, is that the explanation is metaphysical: we are living in a dark age (what he calls the Dark Age) which is seeing the eruption of spiritualities which are the negation of the Uranian, solar spirituality that he favors most. In other words, pop-culture Amazonianism is merely a sign of the times, and there is no one ethnic group foisting it upon us. It is an explanation I myself tend to agree with.

I should note here that a recent trend in the celebrity news media is to dwell obsessively on celebrity pregnancies. The media is in a frenzy of speculation over whether or not Nicole Kidman, or whoever, is pregnant, and stars who are already pregnant receive maximum news coverage. Certainly, 2007 was, in the world of the trash media, the Year of the Pregnant Celebrity. This has drawn protestations from some female journalists, who complain that the trash media seems to think that the pregnancies of these celebrities are more noteworthy than their artistic accomplishments. (I myself think that the artistic accomplishments of the majority of both male and female celebrities in the year 2007 were not very noteworthy, myself – so maybe celebrity pregnancies make better copy than anything Kidman, Heath Ledger, Naomi Watts, Russell Crowe and the rest have done this year).

Related to this is the practice of celebrity adoption, particularly the adoption of children from the Third World. Madonna and Jolie have adopted children from Africa, and, in Madonna's case at least, have removed the child from its birth parents. Africa, of course, is portrayed in the Western media as a continent wracked by war, poverty, famine, corruption, repressive government, and barbaric sex crimes. And, what is more, Westerners – who are, in the liberal democratic discourse, citizens of a globalised world – are obliged to take care of Africa's problems, through aid and peacemaking efforts, but also through adopting orphans from Sudan or wherever, and giving them 'a better life' in the West. Certainly, to judge by their actions, the Madonnas and Jolies seem to think that way. (Likewise, immigration of Africans, on humanitarian grounds, is another form of aid. That is, African immigrants from war-torn, oppressive countries, have the 'right' to a life in the West, to share in its abundance and prosperity).

3. Aphroditism and consumerism

It is a fact that women are very big consumers of luxury consumer goods: that is, consumer goods that we could easily live without – expensive clothes, shoes, home furnishings and the like. Any man who has ever leafed through a woman's magazine, or watched a TV program on women's beauty 'needs,' would draw the conclusion that women's inner thought processes revolve largely around hair and skin care, makeup, diets, the prevention of ageing, makeovers, 'looking good' by buying the right clothes and shoes (and wearing them the right way) and the like. In comparison, men seem to pay little attention to these things: advertising aimed at men, for instance, gives the message that men are creatures whose sole preoccupations are beer, sport, cars and DIY home repairs.

My own conclusion is that the advertisers, magazine editors and others are largely correct: the vast majority of men, and women, are interested in those subjects, almost to the exclusion of anything else. I say this because those advertisers, manufacturers of luxury consumer goods, etc., would hardly be able to make a living otherwise, and they do – the market for women's rejuvenating skin creams, for instance, is huge. Partially, this is all a result of living in a technologically-advanced society where machines do much of the ordinary, hum-drum chores of the household for us. Traditionally, women in the past had to look after the house, and attend to the domestic chores. But they did not have the labor-saving, and time-saving, devices that we have now. Food had to be consumed quickly because there no refrigerators; washing had to be done by hand. Children had to be looked after, with direct supervision, and now the TV functions as a babysitter. Because of automatic dishwashers, the washing machine and all the other domestic labor-saving devices, women who stay at home become bored, and tend to go shopping to relieve that boredom. Which is natural: many shopping malls are pleasant places, and buying a new consumer item – especially a luxury – can generate its own short-lived 'high', just like a cigarette, a cup of coffee, or a win at a poker machine. As a result, the instinct which leads a mother to provide for her children, the hunter-gatherer instinct, is inverted, and turned towards consumerism. And, for adolescent girls, spending on luxury items becomes a competition, fuelled by peer-pressure. They feel compelled to keep up with the likes of Paris Hilton – but do not have the means to keep up, i.e., Hilton's inexhaustible wealth.

In addition to shopping-mall consumerism, another pleasure is the celebrity gossip magazine, covering the dreary trivialities of the lives of Angelina Jolie and Brad Pitt, Tom Cruise and Katie Holmes, and the rest, and the latest sordid escapades of Britney Spears and Paris Hilton. Princess Diana continues to generate news stories almost daily, even though she has been dead for ten years, and obviously, there is a market for every new scrap of information about her. (Incidentally, in my own experience, the majority of people interested in the British Royal Family are female).

The reason why such figures generate such fascination among women is vicarious identification: or rather, women want to be like Angelina Jolie and Princess Diana – they want that money, that luxurious lifestyle, the clothes, mansions, expensive holidays in luxury resorts, and affairs and marriages with handsome wealthy men. They also want to have their cake and eat it, too: that is, they want that lifestyle, and children – hence the media obsession with the pregnancies of wealthy female celebrities. All of this represents an escape from the routine, budget-restricted life: and the fact that the grass is always greener.

There is also an element of drama in the lives of these celebrity women, and danger: did Katie Holmes marry a Scientologist nutcase? Will Brad return to Jennifer Aniston and abandon Angelina? What does Kate Moss see in the out-of-control drug addict Pete Doherty? Will Victoria Beckham drop dead from an eating disorder? The media constantly focuses on scandal, infidelity, marriage troubles, anorexia and obesity, and general drama of all kinds – and where there is no drama and scandal, the media invents.

To a certain extent this is natural. Often, more politically-correct observers are surprised by the extent of two things: a) women's tendency to place other women on a pedestal (e.g. Princess Diana, Jacqueline Onassis, Elizabeth Taylor, Princess Grace of Monaco and other celebrities, who exist on a hierarchical plane far above the masses); and b) women's appetite for luxurious consumer goods. One has to recall the socialist 'queen' of Argentina, Evita Peron, a beautiful woman who clothed herself in expensive furs, wore expensive jewellery, etc. A true socialist should never do such things, but Evita was wildly popular with her constituency - impoverished, lower-class women - who approved of Evita's ostentatious displays of wealth and conspicuous consumption.

Even though we live in a liberal democratic society, the masses still seem to feel the need for royalty, or at least, elevated figures of great wealth, beauty and refinement.

Vicarious identification, and wish-fulfillment, is at the heart of the fascination with the likes of Jolie and Princess Diana. But what of Lohan, Hilton and Spears? No woman would want to be like them, surely? I say this because these women are the unfortunates of the celebrity world: they are always in trouble, always having trouble with husbands and boyfriends, always going on self-destructive, booze- and drug-fuelled rampages (which often lead to arrest). And, not to put a fine word upon it, they are trash – they lack class.

For all her money, Britney Spears is trailer-trash, a lumpenproletarian who celebrated her wedding to the hip-hopping Kevin Federline with a wedding reception at KFCs. In addition, both Spears' and Lohan's careers are in decline: I know, from reading the entertainment pages, that Spears' new album was outsold by a new release by the Eagles, and that Lohan is virtually broke from spending her wealth on drugs, dresses, extravagant holidays, houses, etc. No doubt many women envy the wealth of Hilton, Lohan, Spears (and that of a comparatively minor, but equally self-destructive celebrity, Amy Winehouse); but few would envy their lives. And then there is the question of sexual morality: conventional, conservative sexual morality – which still governs much of our lives – frowns on Hilton and her pornographic videos, etc., and certainly would not approve of a woman in real life who mimicked her behavior, and that Lohan and Spears.

All of this is a kind of rebellion. But, instead of being a political rebellion, it is an individualist one. The energies that would be channeled into activism are now channeled into consumerism, escapism, and debauchery.

In my view, the cult of Lohan, Spears and Hilton is a symptom of what Evola calls 'Aphroditism'. As Evola writes, in a rather sensationalistic passage:

Baumler wrote this, in the introduction to the already mentioned selected writings of Bachofen: "In the streets of Berlin, Paris or London, all you have to do is to observe for a moment a man or a woman to realize that the cult of Aphrodite is the one before which Zeus and Apollo had to beat a retreat...The present age bears, in fact, all the features of a gynaecocratic age. In a late and decadent civilization, new temples of Isis and Astarte, of these Asian mother goddesses that were celebrated in orgies and licentiousness, in desperate sinking into sensual pleasure, arise. The fascinating female is the idol of our times, and, with painted lips, she walks through the European cities as she once did through Babylon. And as if she wanted to confirm Bachofen's profound intuition, the lightly dressed modern ruler of man keeps in leash a dog, the ancient symbol of unlimited sexual promiscuity and infernal forces"... Woman and sensuality often become predominant motifs almost to a pathological and obsessive degree. In Anglo-Saxon civilization, and particularly in America, the man who exhausts his life and time in business and the search for wealth, a wealth that, to a large extent, only serves to pay for feminine luxury, caprices, vices and refinements, has conceded to the woman the privilege and even the monopoly of dealing with 'spiritual' things. ('Do we live in a gynaecocratic society' (1936), translation copyright © 2003 Thompkins and Cariou).

This explains, to my mind, the cult of Lohan, Spears and Hilton – trashy women who lead opulent lifestyles, who have public affairs, make pornographic films and who, despite their lumpen-esque behavior, still occupy a privileged place in our society. They are like the pagan priestesses of the Venusian cults of the ancient world. (It can be said, too, that the explosion of pornography (and nudes in advertisements at newspaper stands, billboards and the rest) in the modern age, especially Internet pornography, is another sign of the resurgence of the cult of Venus, so to speak).

Men are the biggest consumers of all this pornography. But this is precisely the point: they are bound, spiritually, to this cult of Aphrodite, as manifested through ubiquitous pornography, nudity in advertising, etc., which has been created by other men (usually in the United States). They wallow in decadence while their countries, politically and economically, go to ruin. The situation is not so different from that of Germany in the time of the Weimar Republic, when the young men of Germany indulged in 'Aphrodisian' sensuality instead of defending their country against communism, and working to fix their country's myriad foreign policy and economic problems.

4. Women in politics

The reader may point out that here I have neglected to examine another form of Amazonianism: the rise of the woman Statesman. At the time of writing, Hilary Clinton is making a bid for the White House – and many liberal feminists are supporting her campaign, regardless of what her actual policies are, because they feel that 'It's time for a woman president.'

Margaret Thatcher and Indira Ghandi were two women who set precedents for women being Heads of State (and it is no coincidence that Thatcher's propagandists compared her to the British warrior queen, Boudicea, a decidedly Amazonian figure who will soon have a Hollywood film, in the style of 'King Arthur' (2004), made about her). But more interesting is the role that women play in getting male politicians elected. As 50% of the electorate, they play a vital role, of course: but they also, as wives and partners, play a role in motivating men to run for office. One only has to look at the instrumental roles Cherie Blair and Hilary Clinton played in elevating their respective spouses. Some wives, like the former Australian Prime Minister John Howard's wife, and George W. Bush's wife, seem to play a minimal role; others, like Cherie Blair, Hilary Clinton and wives of despots such as Marcos and Suharto, are a driving force.

This is natural, to a certain extent. Wives and female partners often tend to encourage their spouses to achieve more, to do more with their lives, to obtain the respect that they rightfully deserve ('How could you let x work colleague speak to you like that?'), to occupy the station in life that they truly deserve. There are many examples from literature and popular culture (Lady Macbeth being one of the most famous). To a certain extent, this is all healthy, and the consequences are not always as evil as in the cases of Blair, Clinton and Macbeth.

Part of the problem in nationalism is not merely the lack of female members, but the lack of female members who are driving forces in men's lives. Instead of constructive political activism, many men use nationalism as an excuse for drunken get-togethers, where the conversation consists of complaints about the behavior of certain ethnic minorities. Without motivation, without the desire for success and achievement in politics, and all the appropriate skills for success, professionally and in the community, nationalists will accomplish little. They will also fail to attract admiring, supportive spouses.

And this, I think, is one of the many reasons why women are not attracted to nationalism (at least in the Anglo-Saxon countries): they see little in the way of material and social benefit. A woman who is a former trade-union lawyer can achieve a great deal of success in the Australian Labor Party, by simply mouthing all the things that the unions want her to say; but a similar career path, leading to similar success, is not available in nationalism – either for a woman or her spouse.

Having said that, an increase in the number of women members will not cure all ills. One only has to look at the Australian communists, who attract plenty of young women, all right – but women who are, in my experience, bitter and twisted because they feel persecuted against and discriminated against because of their sexual orientation.

One of the other things that women find unattractive about nationalism is, I think, its emphasis on women's role as the progenitors of the white race – specifically, their responsibility as progenitors – brood mares, so to speak. (Both fascism and communism, historically, tended to laud women as child-bearers, homemakers and housewives. Nowadays, of course, women see this as too limiting). While, of course, the majority of women will end up having children at some point in their lives, there are metaphysical types – or what Camille Paglia calls 'sexual personae' – besides The Mother. (Indeed, the image of woman in nationalist propaganda, especially white nationalist propaganda, is often evocative of Demetrian spirituality – the exception being, of course, that the Demetrian, lunar mother type in nationalist propaganda is racialist.

Demetrianism is egalitarian, rejects hierarchy, and treats all people and all races as being equal. Nationalism, of course, does not reject hierarchy, and makes distinctions between the races. Its propaganda emphasizes that it supports the notion of white motherhood, not motherhood in general). Nationalists should, I think, try and give women more options – and not restrict the role of woman to The Mother. After all, we nationalists do not want to produce another generation of bored housewives like those of the fifties, sixties and seventies, who resorted to anti-depressant pills and other legal drugs to relieve their boredom.

The solution? We do not want go down the communist route – communist ideology draws on Amazonian imagery (e.g., women as soldiers, factory workers in overalls and the rest). At the same time, it should be pointed out that fascism, historically, while championing the role of woman as mother, also possessed a modernist, feminist tinge (often overlooked by hostile communist and liberal commentators), making icons out of Amazonian figures like Leni Riefenstahl and Hanna Reitsch. Fascism owed its successes in winning the support of millions of Europeans, and many European women, because, I think, it was flexible in its 'party line' when it came to women.

5. Masculinity in nationalist politics

I was discussing the contents of this article with a friend of mine who is a nationalist intellectual and who writes articles for nationalist publications. I mentioned that I would touch upon the subject of Amazonianism in popular culture. Inevitably, we started talking about a related issue: the subculture of male 'nerds' in the West who are vociferous consumers of American pop culture (especially with a science-fiction or fantasy theme): e.g., films, television shows, comic books, manga, anime, role-playing games, computer games and the rest.

These men, who are often physically out of shape and badly groomed, seem to live in a world of pop fantasy which is completely disconnected from reality. They seem to have little interest in politics or anything else that happens in the real world. They also have little interest in anything which is part of the tradition of 'high' Western culture (that is, novels, films, plays, operas, paintings, or sculpture which is not mass-produced American or Japanese junk). If a film does not have a science fiction or fantasy theme, they will not watch it: trying to sell them on the virtues of classic filmmakers, such as Godard, De Sica, Jean Renoir, for instance, is a futile task.

In the West, the phenomenon of 'nerdism' is ever increasing. From a nationalist standpoint, nerdism is harmful: it is, in fact, a selfish form of consumerism, of liberal individualism, which is about as bad as Paris Hilton, indiscriminate credit-card driven consumerism – in fact, it is probably the male equivalent. Young, impressionable women waste huge amounts of disposable income on shoes to increase their physical allure; young men, 'Warhammer' figures, to retreat from traditional masculine imperatives like finding a mate. (A young man playing a 'World of Warcraft' game can be transformed into a hero – that is, a hero on the Internet. In this, they are not so different from the 'keyboard commandoes' of nationalism, who are heroes on the Internet, but politically ineffectual in real life).

Again, I am not being prudish here: games like 'World of Warcraft' and the like are fun. But these young men are concentrating on these mass-produced entertainments to the point of excluding everything else; and, if they do not concentrate on some of the other problems afflicting our civilization – e.g., the demographic threat posed by immigration – they will, in the end, have no popular culture entertainments left to enjoy. (E.g., the actors in any upcoming fantasy epics will all be non-white; traditional European themes, based on medieval European, and Celtic and Teutonic folklore, will be replaced by Hindu or African ones).

So how do we attract such young men to nationalism? Well, the problem is just that: how to attract them. Why should they want to be nationalists?

The answer is, I think, by appealing to a sense of heroism. Nationalist ideology, at its best, rests on, among other things, confrontations and glorious struggles against our enemies (who are, more often than not, the communists). Nationalist man is very much a heroic, martial man: someone brave enough to march down the street, in a demonstration, and stand side by side with his comrades, waving a nationalist flag and enduring the jeers, screams and provocations of the assembled communist Left who seek to 'smash fascism' by smashing him, physically. Martyrs in the nationalist canon, like Daniel Wreststrōm, are glorified – just like Boromir in 'Lord of the Rings'. (More than a few observers have pointed out the correlation between nationalist ideology and epic fantasy – in particular, their glorification of daring, heroic feats). Nationalism, too, has a place for the physically slight men who are not street fighters – men like Goebbels, John Tyndall and William Pierce – who function as agitators, writing politically provocative speeches and articles, an act which, in our present age of politically-correct anti-free speech laws, carries its own risks. One can say that it takes a certain type of man – a man with guts – to want to become a nationalist. And this, I believe, is how one can appeal to the nerds: by offering them, like the army recruiters of old, the prospect of a life of excitement and danger (while hoping, of course, that none of them meet the end of the unfortunate Daniel Wreststrōm).

6. The Traditionalist rebellion

Fascism, and much of post-war nationalism, has always promulgated the one metaphysical type: the 'heroic', 'solar' type of spirituality. In Evola's writing, the heroic spiritual type as an attempt to regain the primordial Uranian and solar spirituality, lost after the successive waves of distortions and deviations of previous epochs. The heroic epics of Hercules, Gilgamesh and others describe spiritual journeys – not mere adventures – which are quests for that lost, solar spirituality. It is masculine – Evola uses the term virile to describe it – but not the coarse, phallic masculinity of the Titanic type.

Now, this brand of metaphysics is bound to appeal to men in the current age, which is very much a feminized age. I am not talking here of the proliferation of Amazonianism in pop culture, or Aphroditism, etc., but in the structure of our economy itself.

I once read a statistic (which I am unfortunately able to find again and reproduce here) that most of the hundreds of thousands of jobs created in Australia in the last ten or so years have gone to women. Anecdotally, this seems to be the case: in our everyday dealings with the banks, the electricity companies, government agencies like the educational institutions, the hospitals, social security, the Road Traffic Authority and the like, are staffed by young (20s, 30s) white-collar women, who are (again, statistically) more likely than not to be single. Our lives, in the West, have become bureaucratized, thanks to the proliferation of government red tape, rules and regulations for everything, and most of the bureaucrats one encounters in one's daily dealings with the banks, government institutions and the like, are, more often than not, from this class of young white-collar women.

So men are bound to encounter 'bureaucrats' of this type, again and again – dealing with bureaucracy is inevitable in today's world – and certainly, this must have a demasculinizing effect on men over the long term, especially given that our conventional morality tells us that it is a man's responsibility (and a man's alone) to support his wife and his children. That, of course, has changed, with the rise of the single-parent household: but the perception that a man has these moral responsibilities still lingers, and certainly, I know many men still have them. And the question is whether having households without fathers – in Australia, we have 750,000 people on sole parent's benefit, the majority of them being female sole parents – is, socially, good or not. I myself would say no.

So why are there so many women in employment? The answer is, economics – or at least, the economics of the post-1970s period. The inflation of the 1970s - following the break-up of the Bretton Woods system of the gold standard and fixed exchange rates – led to an economic deterioration which was so widespread, and so ruinous, that men were unable to support their wives and children on one wage, as they did in the 1950s and 1960s. So women were forced to go out and work.

The solution to the problem is, of course, economic. In economist's jargon, we need to increase the capital-labor ratio in favor of labor: that is, capital, invested in the market, has to become plentiful in comparison to labor. A bidding war for workers, between rival capitalists, will begin, and wages will go up – which will enable men to support wives and children on one income again. (That is, of course, if that single income will be enough to pay for high house prices (for houses located near the city centers) and the modern consumerist lifestyle. Some would say no, and that a two-income household is necessary to meet such demands).

But, of course, such a solution is nowhere in sight, especially given that incompetents today are in charge of running the economies of the West, as evinced by declining share market values, inflation, high interest rates and all the other ugly economic phenomena.

In the meantime, until the economy is fixed once and for all (and I myself am convinced that, under the system of liberal democracy, the economy will never be fixed, i.e., it will never benefit the good of the wider population but only big business and its shareholders). Instead of purely economic solutions, we need nationalism of the kind described above – one that resurrects the imperial, solar and 'virile' virtues, in defiance of the present depraved age of Aphroditism, Amazonianism and all the anti-Traditionalist spiritualities. Nationalism becomes an act of rebellion.

Subconsciously, I think, the masses are Traditionalist: the 'solar' virtues are what the men and women of the West want. So we nationalists must be prepared to give 'heroism', in Evola's sense, to them.

13

TIBET AND THE LESSONS FOR THE WEST

What does the Chinese occupation of Tibet, and the resistance of Tibetan nationalists against that occupation, have to do with nationalism here in the West? The answer is: a great deal. This article will use the recent events in Tibet as a starting point, and attempt to break down Left-Right thinking on the subject – that is, it will try and show that the Left does not have an exclusive monopoly on the issue. The intention of this article is to show that it is no exaggeration to say that, 'We are all Tibetans now'.

Just as during the time of the Burmese repression of the uprising of the monks, the Left in Australia, in particular the communist groups, are trying to seize hold of the issue, and make themselves look good by associating themselves with the Tibetan uprising. They blame the Chinese heavy-handedness on 'capitalism' (despite the fact that the Chinese Communist Party is responsible for the occupation and repression). Likewise, the liberals are trying to portray it purely as a human rights issue. But the most important element of the Tibetan uprising is the question of national identity, national self-assertion in the face of immigration. And that, of course, relates to us in the West: we are in the same position as the Tibetans.

The article shall conclude with an example of some of the techniques we nationalists can use to foment Tibetan-style national awakenings in our own countries. Really, we nationalists should be ashamed of ourselves: the Tibetans face a greater danger, and face worse persecution, than we do; yet, we are afraid, and, more often than not, too afraid to come out from behind the keyboard.

1. Forced immigration

The Tibetan uprising is an anti-immigrant protest. As the mainstream media reports:

But an influx of Han Chinese to Tibet, and a growing sense among Tibetans that China is irreparably altering their way of life, produced a backlash when Communist Party leaders most needed stability there, analysts say. China has also encouraged huge numbers of Chinese migrants, whose presence has diluted the Tibetan majority... The state media has tightly controlled its coverage to focus on Tibetans burning Chinese businesses or attacking and killing Chinese merchants. No mention is made of Tibetan grievances or reports that 80 or more Tibetans have died... "That is one of the biggest sources of resentment," Mr. Shakya said of the Chinese migration. He said Tibetans believed Chinese were given more opportunities for jobs, and Tibetan unemployment is high. Beijing surely noticed that the younger generation it hoped to entice was rampaging on the streets of Lhasa. ['Simmering resentments led to Tibetan backlash', The New York Times, March 18, 2008].

Immigration here is being used as a weapon. The Chinese, in Tibet, have tried to change the ethnic composition of the Tibetan population by forcing as many immigrants – from China – upon them as possible. Another conspicuous example of the same technique is in the Palestinian Occupied Territories. Israel, for decades, has been trying to change the ethnic composition of the Territories by settling as many Jewish-Israelis there (I use the word 'Jewish-Israelis' as opposed to 'Israeli', because there are one million Arab-Israelis in Israel, and they are not the ones being settled). Recently, the Israeli government announced that it would build 40,000 units (!) for 'young Jewish couples' in occupied East Jerusalem, all this while the "Peace Process" is meant to be going on.

(In fact, the State of Israel itself got started using this method – of deliberate 'over-immigration'. Jewish-Europeans, mainly from Poland and Eastern Europe, settled in Palestine in the hundreds of thousands before, during and after the Second World War. By 1948, the Jewish-Europeans had waged a successful guerrilla war against the British, forcing them out, and had built up enough numbers (and gathered enough material support, i.e., arms from Josef Stalin) to form an army and wage a successful conventional war against Palestine's Arab neighbors. The remaining parts of Palestine were partitioned between Jordan and Egypt, and 800,000 indigenous Palestinians were ethnically cleansed. The new State of Israel was formed, and received diplomatic recognition from both the USSR and USA within hours. The rest, as they say, is history).

Now, the strategy of forced immigration is extremely effective. Why? Because the presence of large numbers of immigrants becomes a fait accompli: it takes cruel, not to say inhuman, measures to get rid of those immigrants once they have arrived, and once they have lived there for a few generations. The Palestinians in the 1920s, 1930s and 1940s, resented, naturally, the huge influx of Jewish-Europeans. But that resentment – which often exploded into riots and acts of violence against the immigrants (similar to what we are seeing in Tibet) – was met with cries of "racism" and "anti-Semitism", even "Nazism". It is notable, too, that the Jewish-European immigrants, and the Jewish Diaspora outside Palestine, exploited Palestinian acts of violence against the immigrants to the hilt, using the incidents in their propaganda war against the Palestinians, just as the Chinese government today is using footage of Tibetan violence (against Han Chinese immigrants) in its propaganda war.

Now, we in the West are in the same boat as the Tibetans and Palestinians. We have not reached the crisis point, but we are getting there. Britain has received hundreds of thousands of new immigrants, following the election of Tony Blair in 1997 (and this is on top of the immigrants from the Caribbean and the Sub-Continent, who arrived in huge waves in the 1950s, 1960s and 1970s). America's Hispanic population has reached 34 million, and threatens to eclipse the Afro-American population in size (10% of the Mexican population has departed for America). Australia has received tens of thousands of Indian and Chinese immigrants in recent years, under the "conservative" government of John Howard, and at this rate, Sydney will be an all-Chinese city in a few decades, Melbourne all-Indian. One could go on, citing the huge numbers of immigrants into Germany, France, the Netherlands, New Zealand and other Western countries.

Because these immigrants have put down roots, it will be a difficult – some pessimists say, impossible – job to remove them. This is not because of "assimilation": from my own experience, the non-European immigrants to Australia have not "assimilated" (i.e., magically become Australian in all respects except the racial) even after living here for decades; likewise for the 3 million strong Turkish immigrant population in Germany. No, repatriation is difficult because of the dislocation and suffering it inevitably entails. The Chinese government, and the Israeli government, know that. Woe betides the Palestinians if they ever became militarily strong enough to force the Jewish-European settlers in the Territories to leave. The Jewish-Israeli religious fundamentalist settlers in Gaza, for example, put on an Oscar-winning performance of grief and suffering (with some sympathetic media coverage) when they were forced to leave by their own government. And now the Chinese government is stirring up nationalistic fervor among its own people over violence committed against the Han Chinese in Tibet. One can imagine, then, the reaction from the Western mainstream media – which is relentlessly pro-immigrant – were a populist politician to be elected in the Netherlands or Britain and start deporting immigrants who had been there for decades. The media would, in its reporting, would give maximum coverage to the suffering and stress of the deported immigrant families (while overlooking, of course, the suffering and stress decades of immigration has caused to the indigenous Dutch and British populations).

The question is, from a demographic point of view, can the Chinese, and the Jewish-Israelis, win? Can they depopulate Tibet, or the Occupied Territories, through immigration? The answer is, I think, no, at least in the case of the Palestinians. There are 3.6 million Palestinians crammed into the Territories: even tens of thousands of new Jewish-Israeli settlers will not make much of a dent.

As for the West: pessimistic white nationalists seem to believe that the European population in the US, Britain, Sweden, Germany, and France are a dying race – that they are in the same position as some Amazonian Indian tribe, who suffer from poor health, low life-expectancy and a low 'replacement rate' (i.e., births replacing deaths). On the contrary, the Western populations are the healthiest and the most long-lived in the world. They will not disappear from the US, or Germany, any time soon. But – and here is the but – they will disappear, in large numbers, from the areas the immigrants are migrating to. The phenomena of 'white flight' are very real, and we are seeing it in action all over the West today. In effect, this is an ethnic-cleansing of the cities (which is where almost all immigrants go). Over time, the numerous numbers of indigenous British, French, and Germans will be pushed out of their capital cities, and replaced by immigrants. The population of the Western nations, overall, will increase, to unsustainable levels – unsustainable economically and environmentally.

The question is - why is this going on? What aggrieves people about the Tibetan, and the Palestinian, situation is the malign intent of the occupiers: China and the Jewish-Israelis are prepared to use force, and immigration, in an attempt to destroy the Tibetans and Palestinians respectively, on every level – culturally, economically, and, in the case of the Tibetans, even environmentally. So what of the governments in the West - do they possess that same intent? Yes, they do. But the strange thing is that the pro-immigration politicians – the Merkels, Browns, Bushes, Rudds – are of European descent, and yet, at the same time, do not seem to like their own people very much. At least, they do not want people of European descent to be in the majority. Why is that?

One of the answers is, simply, that it is a generational thing. The parents of the Bush-Brown-Rudd generation were racialist (without thinking about it too much) and opposed Third World immigration (and, in America, desegregation). That generation fought a long war against their parents – a political and cultural war – against race-based immigration policies, against Apartheid in South Africa, against segregation in the American Deep South. They won that war, or at least, they are in power (and their parents' generation are not any more). And, in their minds, they are still fighting the same struggle today. They dislike their parent's generation and its values so much that they are willing to see their countries disappear under a flood of non-European immigration.

Which, in fact, is a cause for hope: if the next generation of leaders is more nationalist than the Browns and Bushes, we will see a reduction of immigration and a rejection of the state-sanctioned ideology of multiculturalism. In the meantime, we must contend with the fact that our present leaders do not really care about the indigenous populations of Britain, Germany, France, Sweden, and the European populations of Australia, New Zealand, the USA, and Canada. 'Anglo' or 'European' culture is boring, too 'white bread': we need 'diversity,' more and more immigrants, and anyone who voices their objections to immigration is a racist and deserves to go to jail. That is the world view of the 'Generation of 1968', which now rules the entire Western world – through the parliaments, the universities, the opinion columns of the newspapers, through television drama, through film.

2. The ethics of occupation

As anyone familiar with the left-wing scene in Australia knows, the communist groups here are Trotskyist: they have a fanatical devotion to the ideas of Trotsky, no matter how outdated Trotsky's positions have become (after all, he died in 1941). Now, these same communists in Australia (and elsewhere in the West) oppose the Chinese occupation of Tibet on communist, left-wing and Trotskyist principles. But they are hypocritical to do so. After all, Russia, in the Leninist-Trotskyist period, incorporated the 14 or so other countries which made up the Soviet Union by force, and then went on to invade the Baltic States and Poland (where they were thrashed by the Germans and the Poles respectively).

Likewise, Chinese communism appears to be anti-imperialist, and, historically, has lent its support to 'anti-imperialist' struggles all over the world. The ideology of Chinese communism gives the appearance of being, in principle, opposed to the likes of the Tibetan occupation. But this is only a surface impression. Chinese communism has never opposed imperialism, racism, or nationalism on principle: it has only opposed the imperialism, racism and nationalism directed against it – Chinese imperialism, racism and nationalism is fine. This is something that self-proclaimed Maoists in the West have never understood. (Likewise, Vietnamese and Cambodian communism was deeply nationalistic and racialist, while being fervently anti-colonialist, anti-imperialist – i.e., opposed to Western colonialism and Western imperialism).

In the West, there was another form of radical, left-wing socialism which was opposed to foreign imperialism and colonialism while being, at the same time, nationalistic, and racialist: German National Socialism. It may surprise people to be reminded that Hitler's 'Mein Kampf' was an anti-occupation text (Now before all my friends from the ANTIFA jumping up and down and call me a NAZI because I dare to mention 'Mein Kampf, please keep in mind that by just quoting the man doesn't mean that I agree with the author of the book 100%. Hey, I quoted Mao and Che before and you didn't call me a Commie as yet). The ire of the book is not directed, on the whole, against Jewish-Europeans, but against the French, who occupied, at the time of writing, the Saar, the Ruhr and the Rhineland. The French used the traditional techniques of occupying powers – suppression of language, culture and existing customs, and the encouragement of local separatist tendencies – as a means of continuing their war after the war against the Germans. Hitler, in 'Mein Kampf', champions the rights of an oppressed people – the Germans – against a much stronger occupier. But, like Mao and Lenin, he never took up anti-imperialism as a general principle, and of course, supported the dissolution of Poland, in the 19th century, into Germany and Russia (with all the accompanying suppression of Polish customs, language and culture).

That is how it is in politics: the right or wrong of the matter is relative, depending on one's perspective. What matters is this: do you, or do you not, support the occupation of your own country?

Now, Western Europe has been under Allied – American and British – occupation for sixty years. This is a fact. Even though the US military has wound down its military presence in Germany (because of the end of the Cold War, and requirements in Iraq), it still occupies Germany non-militarily. The same can be said of France, the Netherlands, Italy and the other countries which came under the Allied yoke.

How does America occupy these countries? For starters, the German constitution was written for Germany by the occupiers, and expressly forbids, as we know, any expression of German nationalism or independent foreign policy. And then there is the cultural occupation: the endless flood of anti-German books, films, news coverage, court cases (seeking redress for real or alleged German atrocities committed during WWII), plays, comic books, which seek to "educate" Germans as to how bad they are, and how the American (and Russian) occupiers "saved" them from themselves. Then there is the ritual obeisance paid to the Americans by all German politicians of all mainstream liberal-democratic parties.

The situation is much the same elsewhere in Western Europe – in France, the Netherlands, Italy, and Spain. Indeed, each of these countries is "judged," by the mainstream media, the intellectuals and the politicians, on the basis of its conduct during the war: Italy and Spain are "bad" because of Mussolini and Franco; France is highly suspect because of its support for Vichy (and besides which, it threw in the towel too easily after the German invasion of 1940); and so it goes, even though the war ended sixty years ago. This is all the product of an American occupation which influences the way Europeans see themselves: one could call it an occupation of the mind.

And it was all made possible by an American military occupation. Even in the case of the British, the arrival of millions of American troops to the United Kingdom in the Second World War, for preparation for the Normandy invasion, represented an occupation of sorts: their presence there dissuaded the British from cutting a deal with Germany at this point in the war. Francis Parker Yockey, in 'The Enemy of Europe' (in the chapter, 'Three Aspects of the War'), writes that 'England's total war-effort was brought ever more under the direction of the Washington regime, and England, likewise its remaining overseas possessions, was occupied by American troops.

Thereby the Washington regime wanted to ensure that England would not attempt to bail out of the War....'

The problem all this ancient history (and WWII is becoming ancient history) presents for nationalists is simple: once you, as a nationalist, start talking about immigration, and how something needs to be done about the non-European migrants in one's country (e.g., they need to be repatriated), some liberal or communist will call you "Nazi" or "fascist". This is despite the fact that, until the 1970s, neither Germany nor Italy suffered from an immigration problem: both countries were net exporters, not importers, of people, until the period of post-war economic prosperity. But the foes of nationalism are not given to logic and consistency, and so the burden of war "guilt", in Germany, Italy and other Western European countries, weighs heavily, dissuading any nationalist policy of repatriation. This mentality even affects countries which fought against Germany in the war. In a recent news story in the British press, it was revealed that the British government sent mixed-race children (the products of couplings between Afro-American servicemen and indigenous British women) abroad, despite the misgivings that the plan was somewhat "Nazi".

There is, for the Western nationalist, no way of getting around it. The American occupation of the European mind has very real consequences for nationalists.

The Tibetans (fortunately for them) are not burdened with years of Allied brainwashing (only years of Chinese brainwashing, which seems to have been comparatively less effective). And, to their credit, they have made the political choice: they are acting. No doubt there are many Tibetans who do not want to make waves, and want to lead politically passive lives; but there are others who have had enough, and are taking a stand against a superior military and political power, for nationalism and against immigration. This is while we, in the West, who are facing a graver demographic and cultural problem in the long term, prefer to sit back and play with the X-Box.

3. The solution: get rid of fear

Many people in the West agree with the nationalists that immigration is a problem: and many people who are doctors, lawyers, academics, and journalists would speak out against it if they were not afraid. Who is it that scares them? In Australia, it is not multi-culti fanatics in the Labor and Liberal parties; or journalists like Gerard Henderson and Phillip Adams (who are on the mainstream Right and Left respectively, and who both adore immigration). No, it is the communists. Sooner or later in politics, one has to go out, in public, and meet people in one's community, in order to drum up support. Nationalists need to do that: but they are afraid. Most of the nationalists I know spend half of their lives in fear – fear that a communist will, somewhere, take a photo of them and publish it on a website; or that a communist gang will beat them up; or that communists will disrupt a meeting, a march or a rally. In response to that fear, these nationalists tend to operate like a clandestine secret society – like the Freemasons. Meetings are held in secret, as are conferences with other nationalists from interstate. False names are used when meeting other people and (if things keep going down the Freemason-esque path) secret handshakes will be used as well.

The main problem with this approach is that nationalism is not a conspiratorial movement: it can only survive with the oxygen of publicity. Furthermore, nationalists need to build up their confidence in themselves and their ideas. Third, they need to go out and meet the people. So how can nationalists start doing all this?

Communist groups use posters, fliers and brochures to advertise events: usually rallies or, more often, meetings and educational nights at a function room at a local bar. At these meetings and educational nights, communists deliver speeches, or hold a film night, where they show a DVD of Lenin and Trotsky, or Chavez, or Castro, or the Colombian FARC rebels, or whoever. The communists are, in my experience, completely brazen: they will even include the names and mobile names of the organizers down the bottom of the poster. Communists do not live in fear like we nationalists do: despite their "rebellion" against "capitalism", the capitalists (who, according to the Marxist analysis, control the entire Australian political system) do not care very much – at least, not enough to try and phone the bar owner to close down the event, or send some capitalist thugs around to beat the communists up.

What we nationalists need to do is follow the same strategy of booking function rooms and advertising them heavily. The difference is that we shall design posters, fliers, etc., and fill them with "Left" images and slogans (avoiding, of course, the hammer and sickle), supporting traditionally "Left" causes (the occupation of Iraq, Palestine, and Tibet, for example) and, furthermore, we shall post our advertising in the 'Red' quarters of cities like Sydney and Melbourne – that is, the universities, and the bohemian/student parts of town which (in my experience) are targeted heavily by communists in their recruitment drives. All of this is intended to provoke the communists: and it would be a masterful provocation to hold a nationalist educational seminar/DVD night at a function room right in the heart of Red Sydney or Melbourne, so to speak.

What would the communist reaction be? Firstly, shock and disbelief. Secondly, panic: they would tell each other, 'It's a capitalist plot – these people aren't real left-wingers/socialists, they're Nazis, provocateurs working for the government... Make sure that no-one is fooled by their imposture. We don't want young, naive student-types to be sucked in....' Third, the inevitable reaction: 'Fascist/racist/Nazi scum out. Smash fascism!' Communists will turn up to the meeting, with the intention of taking as many pictures as possible, and to break it up, through heckling, and then force.

And this is what we have to be prepared for. Firstly, we shall have a reasonable number of tough, courageous, and physically intimidating nationalists acting as stewards standing by, and ready to pounce at the first sign of a Red attack. Secondly, we shall bar all cameras at the door –

and anyone caught taking pictures will be thrown out of the meeting and have their camera confiscated before they can flee. (There is always a risk that a communist may take pictures with a hidden camera, but that is a chance we will have to take).

Communists can be expected to exert maximum pressure on the owner of the function room to 'not rent it to Neo-Nazis'. In response to that, we shall tell the owner: 'That's nonsense: we are a left-wing, socialist group, and these commies who are trying to close down our meeting are from a rival left-wing faction'. And, if the owner doesn't believe that we are left-wing, we shall show him our Left-seeming posters and stickers. 'Does this look Neo-Nazi to you?'

Inevitably, the communists will win some of the time, and force us to relocate to a new venue. Possibly, we shall be in a situation where we shall never be able to use the same venue twice. Again, this is another chance we have to take.

The advantage of public meetings is just that: they are public, and interested members of the community are able to attend. Some independent-minded younger people may have heard rumors that the nationalist meetings are "fascist" and "Nazi," and will come to see what all this "fascism" and "racism" is about, and be surprised to learn that we nationalists do have some good and reasonable ideas. Over time, we will be able to attract more of those kinds of people to nationalism. What is more, we will get into the habit of communicating our ideas to people outside the usual small clique of nationalists.

Some nationalists may reproach me here for 'giving the game away,' for revealing too much of our plans. My response to that is, firstly, the communist has a complete contempt for our intelligence and abilities; he or she certainly won't have bothered to read this article in full, much less take it seriously. Secondly, the worst thing the communists can do to us is ignore us – to let us hold our meetings and DVD presentations in their Red neighborhoods.

Nationalism will wither and die without the oxygen of publicity. But a communist ignoring a so-called "fascist," "racist," and "Nazi" presence in his midst? Impossible: such a thing has never occurred in the history of communism. Communists can always be trusted to use the same tactics, and react the same way, over and over. They are, in essence, machines, their brains computers programmed with the dogmas of Lenin, Trotsky, Marx and Engels.

The essential thing is that once the communists see that we are not discouraged by their attacks on our meetings, that we can stand up to them, physically if need be, and that we are not afraid – then they will give up. They will simply stop trying. Nationalism will be accepted as another fact of political life.

4. In conclusion

Now, I admit that this seems quite a leap – going from talking about the Tibetan struggle to communism. But the fact of the matter is that our situation in the West has not reached critical mass in the way that the Tibetan situation has: indigenous French, British, Germans, Swedes, Dutch, and European Australians, Americans and Canadians are not rioting in the street, smashing immigrant shop windows, overturning cars, setting fires, and attacking policemen. In order to oppose immigration and globalization, we in the West need to organize politically. And, as soon as one does that, one comes up against the same problem again and again: organized Red bullying which prevents nationalists from exercising their political rights – communist groups which (to make no bones about it) use terror to achieve their objectives. It is not the liberal establishment – the politicians, academics, trade unions, church groups – which are opposing us, using threats, intimidation and force: it is the communists. (Perhaps, if our government was communist – like the one in China – we would be facing rows of policemen, beating our brains out with truncheons and shooting us).

What is holding us back is fear: a fear, which, to my mind, is unreasonable. Yes, there is a danger that we may get photographed, and have our names and addresses posted on the Internet. But that is not the worst that can happen. For one thing, the communists of today are not like those of the thirties: if they come to our meetings to heckle us, and try and break them up, they will not (like in Stalin's day) be bringing coshes, razors, knuckle-dusters, vials of acid and even handguns. We do not risk injury to life and limb. Extreme politics, of any kind, has always carried grave danger to its exponents in the past. Nothing deterred the anarchist Emma Goldman from touring the world and making speeches in halls (to packed capacity), despite the tremendous repression she faced: one has to admire her courage in the face of adversity, an adversity greater than that faced by any Western nationalist c. 2008. So what if a photo of one of us appears on an Antifa website? So what if a newspaper, in some article buried in page 42, calls one of us a "Nazi", a "racist" and a "fascist"? Compared to Emma Goldman, or any Brownshirt or Blackshirt from the 1920s and 1930s, we nationalists have it easy. And compared to the Tibetans, or Morgan Tsvangirai and the MDC in the former Rhodesia, we have it easy.

No doubt, in some charter of human rights (guaranteed by international law), it says that indigenous populations have the right to resist colonization and immigration. So the Tibetans are justified – legally – in doing what they do. So are we in the West: after all, we are being colonized: the massive flood of immigration in Europe, North America, and Australia, is neo-colonialism.

The problem is that, living in a liberal democracy, we have come to expect that certain rights are a given. In truth, they are not: freedom of speech, freedom of assembly, freedom of association, and the right of national, ethnic self-determination for all peoples, are rights that have to be fought for, that have to be won by the fist. No-one recognizes your rights unless you are prepared to fight for them.

White nationalists, on the white nationalist message boards, like to praise the white race for its courage, its daring. But the truth is that we Celts, Teutons, Latins, Norse, and Anglo-Saxons have not displayed that supposed courage for a long time. Indeed, the very thought of speaking nationalist, and racialist, ideas in public frightens us.

In that regard, I want nationalists here in the West to look at the Tibetan example and feel shame. Here are a people (derided as 'yellows' by our supposedly brave, stalwart white nationalists) who are defending their heritage, their culture, their uniqueness, in the face of awesome repression. They are sticking up for themselves, whereas we are not.

Nationalists in the West need to find the courage in themselves to emulate the Tibetans in their courage, their determination, their sacrifice.

www.ingramcontent.com/pod-product-compliance
Lightning Source LLC
Chambersburg PA
CBHW022104280326
41933CB00007B/249